D1592723

A MEASURE
OF UNCERTAINTY

THE EFFECTS OF THE MASS MEDIA

A MEASURE
OF UNCERTAINTY

THE EFFECTS OF THE MASS MEDIA

Dr Guy Cumberbatch

with

Dr Dennis Howitt

BROADCASTING STANDARDS COUNCIL
RESEARCH MONOGRAPH SERIES: 1

JL John Libbey
LONDON · PARIS

HM
258
C845
1989

British Library Cataloguing in Publication Data
Cumberbatch, Guy
   A Measure of Uncertainty: The Effects of the Mass Media - Broadcasting Standards Council research monographs, ISSN 0956-9073; 1).
   Series editor: Dr David Docherty
   1. Society. Effects of television
   I. Title   II. Series
   302.2'345

   ISBN 0-86196-231-1

Published by
John Libbey & Company Ltd
13 Smiths Yard, Summerley Street, London SW18 4HR, England +44 (0)1-947 2777
John Libbey Eurotext Ltd
6 rue Blanche, 92120 Montrouge, France (1) 47.35.85.52

Typesetting in Times by E E Owens & Co Ltd, London SE15 4AZ
Printed in Great Britain by Whitstable Litho Ltd, Whitstable, Kent.

CONTENTS

Other research available from the Broadcasting Standards Council

Review of Research into Public Attitudes in the UK towards Programme Standards
Broadcasting Research Unit

FOREWORD

The Broadcasting Standards Council has decided to launch this series of research monographs in order to promote well-informed discussion about the effects on attitudes and behaviour of the portrayal of violence and of sex in television and on radio. Moreover, the Council seeks to encourage research which takes seriously the British public's attitudes to the moral values which are depicted in the mass media. This series seeks, therefore, to fulfil three purposes: first, to stimulate inquiries which are underpinned by surveys, experimentation or ethnographic research; secondly, to encourage theoretical and conceptual speculation; and, finally, to review previously published and new studies.

The views expressed in these monographs will not necessarily be those held by the Council. Research on the mass-media is inherently contentious; therefore, there is a need for a forum in which opposing arguments can be rigorously expressed. This series will, in part, provide the forum.

Lord Rees-Mogg

I: OVERVIEW OF THE EFFECTS OF THE MASS MEDIA

Dr Guy Cumberbatch

Summary and Introduction

This report provides a "state of the science" review of media effects set in the context of the history of mass communications. Despite regular interest in effects, the pattern of findings across a broad range of issues has been disappointing. Evidence for direct influence is generally weak with many trivial results reported which are themselves controversial.

Mass communications research has been carried out by scholars from a number of different disciplines who seem to operate in a vacuum. Little consensus exists but there is now general agreement that audiences bring to the viewing situation a set of attitudes, values, beliefs and knowledge which lead to considerable variation in how they respond to media messages. This is even true of very young children. In the absence of much convincing evidence of direct influences, mass communication research has shifted from a search for effects to an attempt to understand how "active viewing" operates.

Within the various social problem areas - such as media portrayals of minorities, anti-social and pro-social behaviour - analysis of media content has been popular. Here one finds some overlap between popular concerns and researchers criticisms of the media. Both point out that television has some unpleasant and even unacceptable faces. However much criticism then extrapolates from content studies to argue for probable influences on the audience. Research which has examined audiences is rarely able to demonstrate clear effects of the mass media.

There are various reasons for this. First of all market forces inevitably mean that the media cannot stray too far from audience interests and so will usually reflect the values, beliefs, concerns etc of a substantial body of the audience. Thus teasing out the extent to which the media shape experiences rather than mirroring them is difficult. Secondly many concerns are about problems which are caused by very many factors. Isolating the unique contribution that television makes to problems such as racism or sexism which are deeply embedded in our cultures is exceedingly difficult.

Despite the intrinsic difficulty of evaluating influences of the mass media, precious little research has attempted to address policy questions which broadcasters necessarily face. For example research examining producers' guidelines is virtually non existent. Thus very little is known about the consequences for the viewer of editing out problematical scenes such as graphic detail of violence.

What seems essential is a better understanding of the various concerns that both broadcasters and the viewing audience have. Policy, if it is to be effective, must sensitively represent these. A review of the research knowledge on effects is useful but perhaps what is now needed is a review of research ignorance. What we don't know is probably more important than what we do know.

Context

It would be quite impossible in the space available to attempt an exhaustive review of the effects of the mass media. Not the least of the difficulties is in the sheer volume of published literature. Few reviews provide any sense of this. However one recent annotated bibliography on violence and terror in the mass media listed 784 publications in this area alone (Signorielli and Gerbner, 1988). It is difficult to hazard a guess at size of the literature more broadly concerned with television and behaviour but Pardes (1982) noted over two thousand research publications "within the last ten years". However to this figure one might add the writings of those centrally concerned with the mass media (such as producers, broadcasters, film and TV critics) plus sundry other disciplines centrally concerned with trying to understand individual and social phenomena (such as criminologists, sociologists, psychologists, psychiatrists, anthropologists, political scientists and so on).

Were this not enough, there exists a remarkable lack of consensus among those who research and review media effects about the conclusions which can legitimately be drawn. As one recent textbook (*Milestones in Mass Communication Research* 1983) pointed out:

> As a developing field, the study of mass communication has been particularly unsystematic. Because they come from a variety of disciplines, communication researchers in the past have almost never co-ordinated their efforts or built on the results of previous research. Seldom have they been willing to abandon a theory because someone else's data failed to support it. Many investigations have been carried out simply because there was a substantial amount of money to do so and the public wanted answers to some policy question. (Lowery and Defleur, 1983 p.3)

In fact the position is rather worse than this implies. There is disagreement within the various disciplines (as will be seen) but most importantly a serious rift exists between the disciplines on the very notion of effects. By and large popular concerns about such things as sex and violence, bad language, tastes and standards do not receive much attention in the mainstream mass communications literature. For example in the current *University Microfilms International Catalogue of Doctoral Dissertations on Mass Media and Communications*, some 500 theses are listed between 1985-1987 (UMI, 1988) but only 13 of these are shown under "media uses and effects". Although this somewhat underestimates the actual number of theses dealing with effects, it does give some idea of how this issue is currently viewed.

History

It has become quite fashionable to trace the history of mass communications research by reviewing the conceptual developments from the 1950s which led to the rejection of earlier ideas about mass media effects. For example two standard textbooks by McQuail (1987), *Mass Communication Theory* and Defleur and Ball-Rokeach (1989), *Theories of Mass Communication* both point out that during the 1920s, 30s and 40s considerable assumptions were made of the power of the mass media (especially through propaganda) to influence behaviour. The basic assumptions were that a) media messages are received in a fairly uniform way by every member of the audience and b) trigger immediate and direct responses. As Elihu Katz has reflected:

> We began mass media research with a study of publicity campaigns, that is, an assessment of short-run attempts to influence or to change opinions, attitudes and actions. That research didn't show any dramatic results - nothing like the results that early students of mass communication had anticipated ... they were interested in the process of remote social control, but they didn't find very much of it in the study of campaigns. (Katz, 1988 pp.362-363)

In order to explain the apparently very limited power of the media to change people a number of theoretical notions were developed. Most importantly, in terms of research generated, the problem was turned round. Instead of asking what the mass media do to people, why not examine what different people do with the mass media? This approach, more generally called the "uses and gratifications" approach, soon became fashionable. Among early research was the work of Herzog on the motivations and gratifications of listeners to daily radio serials (Herzog, 1944, 1954) and Berelson (1948) in an intriguing study "what missing the newspapers means" (carried out during a news paper strike). The continuing popularity of this approach is well reviewed by Werner and Tankard (1988) in their textbook *Communication Theories* and in *Media Gratifications Research* (Rosengren, Werner and Palmgreen, 1985).

A second concept which helped to explain the limited effects discovered in the early research was *personal influence*. This emerged independently in a number of studies but notably in the first and classic election study by Lazarsfeld, Berelson and Gaudet (1944) *The People's Choice*. In this the authors noted an unexpected finding:

> Whenever respondents were asked to report on their recent exposures to campaign communications of all kinds, political discussions were mentioned more frequently than exposure to radio or print. (Lazarsfeld, Berelson and Gaudet, 1944 p.150)

This idea of personal influence was developed in a number of studies notably by Katz and Lazarsfeld (1955) in their book *Personal Influence: the role of people in mass communications*. This introduced the idea of 'opinion leaders' who not only diffuse information and attitudes but also act as a barrier to the direct effects of the media on individuals. More generally this approach has developed as an independent field "Diffusion Research" and has been put to much practical use in attempts to introduce innovations (such as new farming practices in the third world as well as in consumer marketing). An account of this tradition is well covered by Rogers (1983): *The Diffusion of Innovations* and by Mahajan and Peterson (1985): *Models for Innovation Diffusion*.

Arguably the thrust of much post war mass communication research was focused on seeking to explain the lack of media effects rather than attempting to pursue possible processes whereby the media may be influential. Thus individual and social differences (in education, sex, race and social relationships) were all thought to contribute to 'selective perceptions' of media content, 'selective memory' for that content and 'selective action' as a consequence of 'selective media exposure'.

With hindsight early notions that the media may have direct substantial effects became somewhat derisively termed the "magic bullet" or "hypodermic needle" model of media effects. As Defleur and Ball-Rokeach conclude:

> The shift from the magic bullet theory to the perspectives of the selective influence theories was one from a relatively simple to very complex conceptualisation. Suddenly, all the factors - both psychological and socio-logical - that distinguished people from one another were potentially intervening variables. (Defleur and Ball-Rokeach 1988, p.195)

So by the late 1950s there seemed a reasonable consensus among mass communication researchers that the media ordinarily had very little direct effect. The best major theoretical account of the state of thinking was provided by Klapper (1960): *The Effects of Mass Communication*. Essentially he argued that the evidence suggests that by and large the mass media do not have any effect on the audience other than to reinforce existing predispositions. He concluded:

> Mass communication ordinarily does not serve as a necessary or sufficient cause of audience effects, but rather functions through a nexus of mediating factors and influences. (Klapper 1960)

Around this time two important pieces of research were published. Both evaluated the introduction of television to children. The first of these was carried out in Britain by Himmelweit, Oppenheim and Vince (1958): *Television and the Child*. This was followed by a similar study (or rather a series of investigations) conducted by Schramm, Lyle and Parker in the United States (1961): *Television in the Lives of our Children*.

The research in both countries covered a lot of ground and makes compelling reading. However despite a number of concerns raised about undesirable effects of television, the conclusions were generally taken to be quite consistent with those of Klapper, Schramm et al who reviewed public concerns about television and advised:

> For some children under some conditions, some television is harmful. For other children under the same conditions, or for the same children under other conditions, it may be beneficial. For most children under most conditions, most television is probably neither harmful nor particularly beneficial. (Schramm, Lyle and Parker 1961 p.13)

The vague circumspection offered by those who had studied television effects did little to reassure the general public who remained concerned about many things. Klapper (1953) had himself attempted to summarise these by conducting a content analysis of popular magazine articles to identify the themes of public debates about children and television. Furthermore, he interviewed "opinion leaders" (jurists, psychologists, educators etc) about their thoughts on children and television as a social issue. He concluded that the main concerns were with the amount of time children spend watching television, the influence that its crime and violence content might have on them and more generally a worry that children were being exposed to an adult world from which they should be protected. Finally a recurrent theme was a desire for "better" childrens television (usually meaning more 'educational' programmes including the classics).

These concerns have probably remained remarkably stable over the decades (although the kind of research evidence as provided by Klapper is disappointingly thin on the ground, see Wartella and Reeves, 1985). However during the 1960s they were encouraged by broader social developments. Not the least of these was the growth of conflict in America. "Beginning in dreams and ending in nightmares, the 1960s felt like a decade running violently out-of-bounds with no way to call 'time'" (Palmer 1989, p.15). Faced with increasingly violent civil disorder (from civil rights, student activism and anti-Vietnam war demonstrations) a wave of assassinations, "skyjack-ings" and inner city riots, many politicians found it convenient to lay the blame for at least some of these troubles at the door of television. Of course Britain was not totally immune from the turbulent sixties nor from similar attempts to explain them. However the importance of the American experience was that it stimulated research into the effects of the mass media, especially through a number of commissions.

The first of these was initiated by President Johnson in 1968 following the serious escalations of inner city riots. Chaired by Milton Eisenhower, the National Commis-sion on the Causes and Prevention of Violence 1969 produced a special task force report of over 600 pages on violence and the mass media (Baker and Ball 1969). Its conclusions were apprehensive:

> We believe that it is reasonable to conclude that a constant diet of violent behavior on television has an adverse effect on human character and attitudes. Violence on television encourages violent behavior and fosters moral and social values about violence in daily life which are unacceptable in a civilized society. (Baker and Ball 1969 p.199)

However the research evidence on which this statement was made was quite limited. On closer examination only 40 pages of the report are devoted to reviews of the available evidence. Moreover only two new research projects were carried out by the commission. One measured violence on television and the other, public attitudes to violence. As Lowery and Defleur commented:

> ... [The conclusions] were marred by an important consideration. They were not inferred solely from the research and summary papers contained in the volume. The Task Force did a great deal of extrapolation and often outran the data; that is, there are many conjectures and suppositions in the conclusions. However plausible they seem, it is difficult to separate them from the research findings.... That is the major flaw in the volume as a whole. (Lowery and Defleur, 1983 p.319)

A number of people were concerned that the commission simply did not have convincing evidence for its claims. In 1969 Senator John O. Pastore (chairman of the Senate Subcommittee on Communications) wrote to the Health, Education and Welfare Secretary Robert Finch:

> I am exceedingly troubled by the lack of any definite information which would

help resolve the question on whether there is a causal connection between televised crime and violence and antisocial behavior of individuals, especially children. I am respectfully requesting that you direct the Surgeon General to appoint a committee... to conduct a study... which will establish scientifically insofar as possible whatharmful effects, if any, these programs have on children. (Cisin et al 1972, p.1)

This letter led to very considerable funding being made available for some "definitive" research. Initially the Surgeon General's Advisory Committee on Television and Behaviour was allocated $1 million but eventually ran to a budget of $1.8 million. The final "report" covered some 2,000 pages in 7 volumes. In total 60 research projects and reviews were carried out for the committee.

The various effects research considered by the Surgeon General's Committee can be conveniently classified as either laboratory based experiments or as field based surveys. After summarising the evidence from each the Advisory Committee concluded:

Thus, the two sets of findings converge in three respects: A preliminary and tentative indication of a causal relationship between viewing violence on television and aggressive behaviors; an indication that any such causal relation operates only on some children (who are pre-disposed to be aggressive); and an indication that it operates only in some environmental contexts. Such tentative and limited conclusions are not very satisfying. They represent sub-stantially more knowledge than we had two years ago, but they leave many questions unanswered. (*Television and Growing Up* Report to the Surgeon General 1971, p.11)

As Brody (1976) commented in a thoughtful and comprehensive review for the Home Office "The report, in other words, was non-committal to the point of evasiveness". (p.12)

There is little doubt that the official report understated the case as far as a number of researchers were concerned. Lefkowitz - one of the researchers involved - wrote to Senator Pastore to complain:

I feel that the committee's conclusions about the causal nature of television violence in producing aggressive behavior are hedged by erroneous statements, are over-qualified, and are potentially damaging to children and society. (US Senate 1972)

The outcome of this and other complaints was that Senator Pastore held further senate hearings to clarify the situation. He asked Eli Rubinstein, the vice-chairman of the Surgeon General's Committee....

(Pastore) You are convinced, as the Surgeon General is convinced, that there is a causal relationship between violence on television and social behavior on the part of children?
(Rubinstein) I am. Sir. (US Senate 1972, p.152)

Ten years later the Surgeon General's Report was updated (*Television and Behavior: Ten Years of Scientific Progress and Implications for the Eighties* Pearl, Bouthilet and Lazar 1982). In this Rubinstein (1982) wrote the introductory comments to the section on violence and aggression but not in stronger terms than the original report. He noted
... the full authenticity of the effect - let alone its power - is still subject to honest disagreement. (p.106)

What is interesting about the update report is the breadth of issues that it embraces. It usefully goes well beyond violence to consider a very broad range of effects. However little attempt is made to integrate these various sections at least in the kind of way that Klapper attempted. Moreover the reviewers are strangely silent on what mainstream mass communications research had found or indeed concluded. One notable exception is a review by Solomon (1982) of health campaigns on television. He wrote "Clarke and Kline (1974) aptly summarise the literature on the effects of the mass media":

Two decades of null findings... had threatened to drown confidence in the power of mass communications under a sea of references to 'reinforcement' and 'selective exposure'... (cited by Solomon 1982, p.309)

There are a few other points worth making about *Television and Behavior* (1982). First of all, despite the very broad terms of reference accepted for the review, no technical report was commissioned on pornography. An earlier commission (the United States Commission on Obscenity and Pornography) had reported in 1970. It concluded:

Extensive empirical investigations, both by the Commission and by others, provides no evidence that exposure to or use of explicit sexual materials play a significant role in the causation of social or individual harms such as crime, delinquency, sexual or non-sexual deviancy or severe emotional disturbances. (p.58)

This report was rejected by both the US Senate and President Nixon. In 1985 the US Attorney General appointed a new commission to examine issued of pornography and obscenity. It reviewed the available research evidence to conclude that a causal link did exist between exposure to violent pornography and aggressive behaviour towards women.

The omission of pornography from the 1982 review is a pity in that essentially similar problems for research exist in studying pornography as occur in studying violence. An additional point about the 1982 review is that the report is suffused with far more sophisticated theories about media effects than are even hinted at in the earlier Surgeon General's Report. As Singer noted in his introductory comments:

> Today, psychology regards the human being as playing an active and selective role in how he or she approaches each new environment. There is much greater emphasis on the fact that individuals bring to each environment pre-established schema or what might be called "preparatory plans", based, of course, on previous experience as well as fantasised anticipations about what may be expected in a situation .... some of our schema are more complex, more integrated or organised and differentiated from others. (Singer 1982, p.2)

This sounds reminiscent of the conclusions of early mainstream mass communications research. It echoes Schramm's preference for a uses and gratifications approach and his reservations about the effects tradition to studying television's influence:

> .... it suggests that television 'does something' to children. The connotation is that television is the actor; the children are acted upon. Children are thus made to seem relatively inert; television relatively active. Children are sitting victims; television bites them. (Schramm, Lyle and Parker 1961, p.1)

None of the above is to dismiss concerns about potential harmful effects of the mass media. However aggregate approaches which seek to find a direct relationship between television content and social behaviour can be quite misleading - at the least in the eyes of many contemporary researchers. The criticism is not simply that there are individual differences in response to the media but that the starting point for almost all effects research rests on a set of assumptions which are not supported by the facts.

Glued to the box?

The first challenge to these assumptions is of course to be found in early mass communication literature - little evidence was produced that the media have any effect. Among other bits of evidence that helped explain this was the role of opinion leaders. More recently there has been a growing challenge to the idea that people are "glued to the box" when watching television. Half of the time the television is on the audience is doing something else. This literature is well reviewed by Gunter and Svennevig (1987) *Behind and in Front of the Screen*.

This kind of research has only recently attracted public attention - largely through the publicity given to British researchers Collet (Collet and Lamb 1986) and

Svennevig and Wynberg (1986, Svennevig 1987) who video recorded what people do when they watch television. However the approach is quite old. Allen (1965) photographed audiences watching television and found they were inattentive as much as half the time. Bechtel, Achelpohl and Akers (1972) came up with similar findings - in this study talking was the most common other activity. Thus while television may provide a focus for family activities, viewers are not the soporific morons sometimes claimed. Anderson and Field (1985) conclude: "...families incorporate television into their lives in highly individual ways... Television forms part of a complex family ecology ...". (Anderson and Field 1985, p.22)

The second assumption prevalent in many critical approaches to television is that, if people (especially children) were not spending their time in front of the box, they would be doing more valuable things. As Roald Dahl put it: "Oh books, what books they used to know. Those children living long ago!" (Dahl, *Charlie and the Chocolate Factory*)

Similar arguments against television are forcibly made by Milton Shulman (1973) *The Ravenous Eye;* Jerry Mander (1980) *Four Arguments for the Elimination of Television*; Marie Winn (1977) *The Plug-in Drug*; Martin Large (1980) *Who's bringing them up?*; Neil Postman (1983) *The Disappearance of Childhood* to name but a few.

However, reading is one of the few areas on which some research consensus seems to exist: television usually does not seem to have a detrimental effect on childrens reading:

> A negative impact of television on reading has seemed intuitively obvious to many parents and teachers. However reviews of studies investigating the relationship between time spent viewing and reading performance... have noted the research is limited. Generally no clear relationship between the two factors has been found. (Ball, Palmer and Millward 1986, p.132)

The most popular conclusion is that children who watch moderate/average amounts of television may show better reading performance than light viewers but that heavy viewers often do worse on reading performance measures (Beentjes & Van Der Voort 1988; Neuman 1988). However some years earlier Morgan (1980, 1982) was surprised to find that: "Television viewing exerts a significant positive, longitudinal influence on time spent reading, and no causal influence from early viewing time to later viewing is apparent". (Morgan and Gross, 1982 p. 84) Essentially "...those who are the heavy viewers in early adolescence read more in later adolescence". (Morgan and Gross p. 85)

More generally television viewing does not seem to have had any reliable effect on overall educational achievement. Ball et al (1986) list 13 studies which have investigated this. Most (9) conclude there is no evidence of any relationship while 4 suggest slightly negative effects accounting for a few percentage points in school achievement. In an earlier but more extensive review Morgan and Gross (1982) observe a few studies claiming positive effects, a few negative ones but most find no relationship with television viewing: "In sum there is no one effect of television on achievement, nor is there even one relationship". (Morgan and Gross, 1982 p. 83)

Part of the reason for the apparently trivial influence of television on educational attainment is that television does not have much impact on "educational" activities. Much of the time created to watch television is taken from essentially time wasting activities - watching traffic go by and so on. Other time is shaved off a wide variety of activities. Bogart (1972) reviews the various literature on displacement effects of television. As Belson found in the UK, the initial impact of television's introduction is to decrease radio listening, cinema attendance, magazine reading and social activities outside the home (Himmelweit and Swift, 1975). However with the exception of radio (Sterling, 1984) and cinema (Docherty, Morrison and Tracey, 1987) most activities seem to recover. Even though the impact of television looks to have had a massive effect on reducing cinema attendance, it has been argued this may be due to a shift from public leisure pursuits to domestic ones over years rather than to any direct impact of television per se. (Docherty, Morrision and Tracey, 1987)

Other evidence on the displacements effects of television came from a number of studies where people have been deprived of television. In reviewing these Winnick (1988) points to various methodological problems in most "experiments" which are rather anecdotal and are confounded by the problem that those who volunteer to give up their sets may be resolved to change their leisure patterns. Winnick's own research is more convincing in dealing with cases where television was unexpectedly unavailable (after hurricanes and during strikes and in countries where television is unavailable on certain days of the week). This research tends to confirm previous conclusions:

> ...only a handful of the households attempted any systematic program which would provide substitute activities for members of the household in the absence of the television. Hardly any parents developed alternative activities either for their children or for other members of the family during the period of deprivation. (Winnick 1988, p 228)

Barwise and Ehrenberg (1988) argue that television is a low involvement, passive activity which is not likely to be substituted by high involvement active ones, and Christopher Dunkley has argued:

> It is an absurd upper middle-class fantasy to imagine that if only people could be induced to turn their television set off they would all start reading Solzhenitsyn and going to Covent Garden or attending lectures on the late

Renaissance. Most people deprived of their television pick up the *Sun* or listen to Radio 1. (Dunkley, 1985)

All of the above research literature provides an important context in any search for media effects: the studies seem to offer a desert of inconsequential trivial findings. Mining in this desert is not a promising one for discovering significant nuggets of experience or behaviour shaped by the television experience. Perhaps it is not surprising that an increasing research effort has gone in to exploring the varieties of individual reactions to television with an increasing emphasis on the "active viewer" as an explanation of why so little of consequence has been discovered (e.g. Taylor and Mullan 1986; Lindolf 1986; Palmer 1986; Messenger Davies 1989; Silverstone 1989). A very useful up-to-date overview of this kind of research is provided by Brown (1989). Nevertheless general and specific concerns about television remain deeply embedded in public debates and there is no shortage of research which has begun with the apparently reasonable assumption that television simply must do something to viewers. One of the most recurring types of research has involved examining the content of television to determine patterns of messages which it is argued should shape the activities, values and behaviours of viewers. Although not confined solely to one theoretical tradition, much of this work has been stimulated by ideas developed in the United States by George Gerbner and his colleagues at the Annenberg School of Communications in Philadelphia. For convenience the following sections dealing with more specific content related effects will begin with this work.

Specific Effects

In the 1970s George Gerbner developed a new model for analysing the impact of television on society. He argued television's main influence was one of enculturation: that is television's content conveys ideas about social behaviour, social norms and social structures. The more people watch, the more their socio-cultural beliefs will be affected. The approach taken by Gerbner focussed on the "symbolic messages" of television. These are revealed by coding the content of television drama ("message system analysis"). At its simplest level for example the high frequency of violence on American television should provide a message: "The world is a violent place". Messages such as this Gerbner argued should encourage heavy viewers to become fearful that the world is a violent one. This is examined by public surveys ("cultivation analysis"). The theory has much to commend it and is a rich one. Gerbner extended his theory about the likely consequences of "enculturation":

Fearful people want - demand protection and accept, if not virtually welcome, aggression in the name of safety..Fear invites aggression that provoke still more fears and repression. The pattern of violence on TV may thus bolster a structure of social contrasts even as it appears to threaten it. (Gerbner, Gross, Signorielli, Morgan and Jackson-Beeck 1979 p 180)

Gerbner's approach appealed to many researchers at a number of levels. First of all the approach could be logically extended to examine the impact of television in a number of social problem areas - such as sexism and racism where similar concerns exist that television may cultivate negative views. Secondly it appealed as a possible way of demonstrating media power even though this has failed to emerge clearly in so much research studying behaviour. Thirdly the theory appealed to many mass communication researchers whose ideological perspective was firmly rooted in a belief that the mass media performed what was essentially a political role. For them Gerbner's claim that:

Television is the mainstream of (the) cultural process. It is an agency to maintain, stabilize and reinforce - not subvert - conventional values, beliefs and behaviours. (Gerbner et al 1979 p 180)

touched a receptive Marxist chord. Television was the barrier to working class revolution.

Considering the attention Gerbner's work has received, simple summaries of the research evidence are not easily made. At the end of the day the problems lie in the sheer complexity of teasing out the unique effects of the media from the mass of other influences on people's lives. As an overview Wober and Gunter (1988) in *Television and Social Control* provide the best available analysis of the research literature. The problem is simply illustrated - light viewers of television tend to be middle class and live in areas which have lower crime rates than heavy viewers. Middle class viewers tend to watch less crime drama so any association found between attitudes to violence and viewing behaviour is confused (or in statistical jargon "confounded") by these other variables. Television may not be the cause of heavy viewers perceiving the world as more violent - such a belief may be anchored in the reality of their neighbourhood. Additionally as Zielman has argued, people who may be anxious about crime may like to watch crime drama where forces of law and order prevail (Zielman 1980). All in all while there is a fair amount of literature supporting Gerbner's ideas, there is some doubt as to whether the data shows a causal effect of television.

This introduces a more general point that Gerbner's thesis rests on the kind of assumptions which stimulated early approaches to media research. It does not make allowances for differential effects due to individual differences in "active" watching which are now well documented. Of course it is very difficult to resist the idea that the viewing public should share similar reactions to any particular programme but

13

predicting these seems a rather uncertain business. Although these days many researchers argue that one cannot extrapolate from television content to the received experience of the viewer (which needs to be studied as an experience), studying media content has long been popular. It's interesting to note that one of the people who popularized content analysis - Berelson - had himself concluded that mass communication research was a dying field simply because so little success had been shown in finding any effects of the mass media (Berelson 1959).

At this stage it is tempting to continue this discussion with a further consideration of violence but this issue is far from easily summarized. An overview is presented later in this section and a more exhaustive critical review attached (Violence and the mass media). For the moment it would be useful to consider various research on stereotyping of minorities in the media. A number of useful reviews now exist. Most recently Durkin (1986), Greenberg (1986) and Wober and Gunter (1988) have prepared useful summaries while Signorielli (1985) provides a fairly comprehensive annotated bibliography: *Role portrayal and stereotyping on television.*

1 Women and Sex Roles

With the development of the women's movement and concerns about sex role stereotypes, this field has generated an enormous literature on media content. Fortunately, for purposes of review, there seems general agreement that women have been under-represented and negatively portrayed. This seems true across a wide range of media studied in various countries.

Probably more research has examined advertisements than any other medium (see Bretle & Cantor 1988 for a recent review). For example Knill et al (1981) analysed 1600 television commercials to conclude that over 80% of female product representatives were shown in family/home occupations whereas nearly 70% of male product representatives were depicted as having business or management occupations. Moreover 90% of the voice overs ("the authoritative" comment) was provided by males. Although the actual proportions vary a little from study to study essentially the same results emerge in British studies (e.g. Livingstone and Green 1986, Harris and Stovard 1986). The feminist perspective is of course to object that women are shown either as housewives or mannequins and not as career people. This is a reasonable concern especially given the apparently low status of women in society (Equal Opportunities Commission 1988). However, as Scott (1975) pointed out in a study of women's magazine advertisements, the role portrayed tends to be product specific. Thus advertisements for male cosmetics also tend to show men as mannequins.

Although less clear cut, content analyses of dramatic fiction reveal similar patterns.

14

Signorielli (1984) reported that from 1969 to 1981 women were generally out numbered by men by 3 to 1 on American television. Variation over time was small. Even in soap operas where women are more prominent, they are largely subordinate to males (e.g. Greenberg et al 1980). In some genres (adventure and children's television) the sex role stereotyping appears stronger than in others. Even in quality American children's television (e.g. *Sesame Street, Mister Roger's Neighbourhood*) males tended to show achievement, ingenuity, mastery etc while females tended to be passive and helpless. (Dohrmann 1975)

In a sense conclusions are all too easy. However while content analysis may reveal an unacceptable face of television, just how media images affect people is, of course, an empirical question. Unfortunately precious little research has been done on this.

One useful starting point is reported by Wober (1981) and Gunter (1984). They asked a quota sample of adults various questions about men and women "as they appear on television" and as they "actually are in real life". They conclude that viewers do make distinctions and so are unlikely to accept television as a window of the world. Similar conclusions were reached by Scott (1975) in her study of women's magazine advertisements. More recently McCauley and Thangavelu (1988) concluded that their results "...do not support the claim that TV is responsible for distorted social perceptions". (p.197)

One of the strongest pieces of evidence that television may influence sex role stereotypes comes from Morgan (1982). This study of American adolescents found heavy viewers were more likely than light viewers to agree that men are ambitious, that women are happiest raising children and so on. However interestingly, girls who were heavy viewers seemed to develop higher educational and occupational aspirations than light viewers - a curious anomaly. In a review of the various studies attempting to tease out the effects of television Durkin (1986) acknowledges the concern but considers the evidence does not allow very confident conclusions. As Wober and Gunter (1988) also conclude "viewers come to see what they see, and interpret what they see, both in the light of their own preconceptions, and also as reinforcement for such notions". (Wober and Gunter 1988, p 125)

Despite the lack of any clear evidence that television shapes conventional sex roles, this is not altogether surprising given the extent to which these roles are deeply embedded in our cultures. The day to day example of parents where usually clear conventional sex roles are adopted (Equal Opportunities Commission 1988) would provide an important primary experience for children. For example Jowell et al (1988) note that only 8% of the general public said repairing household equipment was a shared activity (82% said the man mainly did it) whereas washing and ironing was shared by only 9% (88% said mainly women did it). Nevertheless it is worth considering experiments which have examined the influence of counter-stereotyped television programmes. Unfortunately these all suffer from the risk of artefacts which are inherent in experiments: when a nice experimenter asks children to watch a film and then asks for their attitudes, children may well be "influenced" by the film content in ways which have little bearing on their usual responses to broadcast material.

With these reservations in mind it is worth considering the American television series *Freestyle*. This was designed to convey counter stereotyped messages in an entertaining format. A total of 13 half hour programmes were produced aimed at 9-12 year olds. A number of researchers were involved in making the programmes (Williams et al 1981) and in evaluating them (Johnston and Ettema 1982). A large experiment (involving 7,000 children) had children either:
a) watch the programmes at school and discuss them with the teacher ("viewing/discussion group") or
b) watch the programmes at school ("viewing/school group") or
c) simply encouraged the children to watch the programmes at home ("viewing/home group").

Childrens sex-role beliefs, attitudes and interests were measured before and after the series. The viewing/discussion group was by far the most effective showing a broad pattern of greater acceptance of counter stereotyped views (eg. about girls who display independence, assume leadership and about boys who engage in nuturing activities). These effects even remained statistically significant in a sub-sample tested a month later. The viewing/school group showed some changes in the same direction but these were weaker and less prevalent while the viewing/home group showed only a few limited results in line with the overall goals of *Freestyle*. Here only the heaviest viewers showed a change on only one measure out of 20.

These findings concur well with the broad pattern of results in mass communications: media influences tend to vary between being weak to non-existent in natural settings unless other things happen. Other things include " pretest sensitization" (eg. measuring peoples attitudes then asking them to watch a film presenting different attitudes) or "reinforcement" (such as follow up discussions). More formal experiments (as in laboratory style approaches) claim rather more success in producing attitude change. There are a number reporting positive results using films of counter stereotyped roles, but the desired changes did not always emerge while several studies have obtained non-significant results or mixed outcomes (Durkin 1985).

Unfortunately most studies launch into a perceived social problem without much attempt to appreciate how children understand sex roles or television. As Durkin (1984) showed even very young children (from the age of 4) when talking about television sex roles refer to real world social conventions and move easily beyond the information given in films to explain their understanding of what's happening.

2 Race and Racism

The history of race and the mass media is a long one. In 1827 the first newspaper for Black Americans was launched: *Freedoms Journal*. In its first issue it proclaimed "from the press and the pulpit we have suffered much by being incorrectly represented" and "Too long have the publick been deceived". Similar complaints have been voiced with each new medium (Cumberbatch 1988).

As with sex roles the vast majority of studies involve content analyses of the media to support their arguments and then extrapolate to suggest the likely effects on the media audience. Few studies address audience issues directly. Studies of content are now well documented (eg. Greenberg 1986, Signorielli 1985). The two largest studies have been decade long studies of television entertainment. Seggar et al (1981) took samples from television from 1971 which gave a data base of some 18,000 characters. Over the decade white males increased from 81% to 88% of all television male characters while black males fluctuated from 6% in 1971 to 9% in 1980 (the same as in 1975). Black females represented 5-6% of all females over the decade. (In the US population blacks represent approximately 12%).

Similar findings were made by Gerbner and Signorielli (1979) based on the decade beginning 1968. Blacks averaged 8% of all characters - a figure confirmed by Weigel et al (1980). More importantly the appearance of black people was more likely to be in minor or supporting roles. Thus, as a proportion of major roles, the figure is lower. Black males accounted for only 4.4% of major male roles whereas black females comprised only 2.4% of all major female roles. Baptista-Fernandez and Greenberg (1980) suggested that these data gloss over a clustering effect: nearly half (41%) of blacks appear in television programmes in groups of four or more black characters. This they argue is a undesirable "ghettoisation" of minorities. Similar data was reported by Barcus (1983) who reported that in 82% of childrens programmes, white and minority children never appear together.

Arguments that television stereotypes ethnic minorities continue but the evidence for this has declined over the years. Following the growth of civil rights in America and notably after the riots of the 1960s

> ...significant changes in both recognition and respect blacks were accorded on television....whereas they had been cast as entertainers, servants or buffoons during their rare appearances in the 1950s and early 1960s a decade later they were more likely to be cast as 'regulators' of society typically playing such roles as teachers or policemen. (Liebert and Sprafkin 1988 p.190)

This may be equally true in Britain but the most recent content analysis dates back a decade (Anwar and Shang 1982) and relies for its argument more on illustration than hard facts.

The major British study was carried out even earlier (Hartmann and Husband 1975). This was a sophisticated piece of research focussing on childrens knowledge of ethnic minorities and attempting to understand to what extent these were influenced by personal experience or by the mass media. The authors found that personal experience seemed to have negative influence on attitudes to "coloureds" but that:

> ...the media do not seem to have any direct influence on attitudes as such. It would appear that the media serve to define for people what the dimensions of the situations are. How they feel about the situation, thus defined would seem to depend on other factors, particularly where they live. (Hartmann and Husband 1975 p.108)

As with counter-stereotyping of sex roles, programmes are made which attempt to reduce racist attitudes. One of these, *Till Death Us Do Part*, attempted to make fun of bigotry personified by Alf Garnett. Vidmar and Rokeach (1974) attempted to assess the impact of the American version of this series (*All in the Family*) on adolescents in the USA and Canada. Both prejudiced and unprejudiced adolescents saw the programme as funny and enjoyable while the bigoted character (called Archie Bunker in the American series) was the most admired of the characters shown. The majority thought that it was wrong to use derogatory words like "coons" and "chinks" but nevertheless saw Archie Bunker as a winner and sympathised with him to a marked degree. Both Brigham and Giesbrecht (1976) and Willhoit and de Bock (1976) carried out similar studies to show racial prejudice was related to liking Archie Bunker and agreeing with his views. This problem of selective perception is a common theme in mass communications research. Poindexter and Stroman (*Blacks and Television: a review of the research literature* 1981), conclude: "...more than 30 years of the published empirical literature provides a dismally incomplete picture of blacks and television."

3   Age and Ageism

Concerns over the portrayal of elderly populations have only more recently become evident in the research literature. However from the early 1970's there have been a large number of studies carried out in America. The most complete bibliography is provided by Signorielli (1985) who also reports one of the largest content analyses of age (Signorielli 1984) based on 14,037 TV characters between 1969 and 1981. She concludes that both the very young and the elderly were under-represented in prime-time dramatic fiction. Older characters were less likely to be presented as 'good' but less likely to be involved in violence than younger characters. Older men were

18

more likely than younger men to be cast in a comic role, while elderly women tended to be shown as unsuccessful and as victims than successful. More importantly around 70% of older men and 80% of older women were judged to be held in low esteem and treated discourteously.

Greenberg et al (1980) report an analysis of nearly 4,000 characters in network fictional series reaching rather similar conclusions. Although older characters were more likely to be verbally aggressive, they were much less likely than other age groups to be physically violent. Part of the reason for this is that older characters are much more likely to be found in situation comedies than in other programme types (especially crime drama).

A number of findings have pointed to more positive images; Gerbner et al (1979) found that loneliness among the elderly is less common than among other age groups while most elderly characters were portrayed as useful. Petersen (1973) reported that the majority of older characters in her content analysis were "active", "in good health" and "independent". Older women in soap operas are generally portrayed in a positive way. (Ansello 1978; Barton 1977; Downing 1974; Ramsdell 1973) Similar conclusions were reached by Dail. (1988)

The only British research completed on television portrayals of the elderly (by members of the University of the Third Age) concurs that the elderly are under-represented but that the roles they portrayed and the treatment they received were largely positive (Lambert, Laslett & Clay 1984). Wober and Gunter (1982) report survey data in Britain on attitudes to the elderly (which were generally positive) and linked these to viewing behaviour. Heavy viewers seemed to have more positive attitudes to the elderly even when age of the viewer was taken into account.

Although there is a dearth of research evidence on effects, the concern that television fosters negative attitudes to the elderly does not seem to receive much empirical support.

4   Disablement

The rehabilitation literature has regularly carried articles criticising media portrayals of disabled persons. However most argue by examples and rarely offer the kind of objective analysis required for serious consideration here. A British review of the issues is well covered by Anne Karpf (1988 *Doctoring the Media*). An extensive review and content analysis of the portrayal of disablement on British television is nearing completion (Cumberbatch et al *Images of Disablement* forthcoming).

As with earlier minority issues, the central complaint has been of under-representation and negative stereotyping (eg. Donaldson 1981; Leonard 1978). Even where positive portrayals occur these were seen as unfortunate (such as tales of heroic struggle to cope with disabilities - Donaldson 1981). However the two most recent American content analyses of television have found that portrayals of disabled/ handicapped persons are most often neutral (Elliot et al 1983; Warzak et al 1988) although there is general agreement that they occur far more infrequently on television than in the general population. (Similar conclusions are likely to be drawn in the forthcoming Cumberbatch et al study.)

So far there does not appear to be any published literature on audience responses to and perceptions of such television portrayals. However a number of studies have used films or videotaped productions in experimental studies in an attempt to improve attitudes to the disabled. These have enjoyed some mixed success but suffer from crude designs and measurement which make interpretation difficult. Many of the problems are associated with the standard measure - Yuker's (1966) Attitudes Toward Disabled Persons Scale - which taps prejudice towards disablement by way of general questions about "disabled persons" without defining the term. Attitudes that people hold will depend much on how they define disabilities which seem never explored in the studies. Obviously "disability" can cover a wide variety of impairments. Showing a film of say a blind person may merely cause audiences to re-define their concept of disability to focus on this particular impairment (since this is what the experimenter seems to be interested in). These and other problems such as pretest sensitisation - giving people a test before the experiments - are likely to result in quite serious artefacts (eg. Matkin et al 1983).

5 Alcohol

In the last two years considerable attention has been given to alcohol abuse as a "new" social problem. The Royal College of Psychiatrists (1986), The Royal College of General Practioners (1986) and the British Medical Association (1986) each produced their own report on the medical, social and psychological dangers of alcohol abuse. Hard on the heels of these reports came the Wakeham Committee's report *Young People and Alcohol* followed by the discovery of lager louts. Although television has not been indicted by many in the recent debates, concerns about the extent to which the media promote alcohol consumption are scattered throughout the various discussions. The Royal College of General Practioners commented:

> The fact that there are individual and societal costs of alcohol as well as benefits is sometimes neglected in media coverage of alcohol related issues, which often concentrates on 'alcoholics', thus perpetuating that unhelpful myth of 'two populations of drinkers' - them and us. (Royal College of General Practioners 1986, p.51)

The British Medical Association argued:

> Images of young and adult drinkers in the media portray them as glamorous and adventurous, but never drunk (except as figures of fun). Alcohol is shown to increase virility, sociability, toughness and maturity. It is depicted as an almost magical tranquilliser. (British Medical Association 1986, p.15)

Fortunately over the last decade or so a number of studies have been carried out to determine the extent and nature of media portrayals of alcohol use. The earliest studies were in the United States: Dillin (1975) (who contributed 3 articles in the *Christian Science Monitor*); Hahneman and McEwen (1978); Garlington (1977); Greenberg (1980) and Lowry (1981). More recent studies have been conducted by Breed and Defoe (1984); Futch et al (1984) and Wallack et al (1985, 1987). Similar pieces of research are now available from Australia (Casswell et al 1983); Scandinavia (Nowak 1982, 1986; Montonen 1985); Poland (Gajlewicz 1986); Chile (Naveillan et al 1987) and Britain (Hansen 1984, 1986, 1988a,b).

The pattern of findings is essentially the same across the various studies: alcohol is the most prominent beverage consumed on television, it is associated with rich luxurious settings and pleasant social interaction. Very little coverage is provided of the negative consequences of drinking. In Britain the popular 'soaps' *Eastenders* and *Coronation Street* with their public house foci produce an impressive rate of alcohol consumption per hour compared with other television drama. Hansen (1988a) notes the differences between series originating from different countries: in Australian series alcohol was consumed at a rate of 7 units per hour; American series ran at 11 units while British series ran at 27 units per hour!

Gerbner's cultivation hypothesis discussed earlier was tested in a fairly cursory way by Gerbner et al (1982) who classified those surveyed simply as drinkers or non drinkers. Surprisingly, overall, the heavy viewers of television were less likely than light viewers to consume alcohol. However when account was taken of demographic and other relevant differences it did not seem that alcohol consumption was causally related to television watching.

In Britain, Wober (1986) carried out a similar study also finding a negative relationship between alcohol use and television viewing. Additionally attitudes towards the merits or otherwise of alcohol were unrelated to viewing of either BBC or ITV (during the period researched alcohol was 14th in the top 20 product categories advertised). Conclusions from these studies would have to be extremely tentative.

The most sophisticated study carried out has recently been completed by Hansen (1988b) in Britain. The design, while seeking effects in a similar way to Gerbner, focuses on the ways in which viewers use, interpret and make sense of television images of alcohol. This involved a survey of 345 young people (12-17 years old) plus a series of focused group interviews with over 100 adolescents. In the various measures concerning alcohol (self reported behaviour, attitudes to abuse etc) no association appeared with amount of television viewing. The young people overestimated the proportion of non-drinkers in the population (compared with official statistics). However there were no differences between heavy and light viewers.

The only support Hansen finds for Gerbner's cultivation theory is very weak: that within particular subgroups of light viewers there was more variety in beliefs about drinking in the United States than there was within subgroups of heavy viewers. This Hansen suggests may point "to the homogenising influence of television on viewers beliefs about those aspects of alcohol consumption which cannot be readily checked against personal experience or direct observation" (Hansen 1988, p.x) The most valuable contribution of Hansen lies in his use of group discussions which reveal in a qualitative way what viewers think (or at least say they think).

Perhaps the most interesting were the young people's response to the quite different portrayals of alcohol abuse by Sue Ellen in *Dallas* compared with Angie in *Eastenders*. Despite the constructed nature of *Dallas* and stereotyped skid row image of "the alcoholic" that Sue Ellen comes close to, the young people found it more convincing than the more realistic image of Angie. In terms of current thinking about alcohol abuse (as given by *Alcohol Concern*) everything about *Dallas* was wrong in encouraging the popular view of two populations "them" who are alcoholic and "us" who can drink safely. Sadly the potential that *Eastenders* had to educate and inform seems - like so many mass media messages - to have missed its mark at least on this occasion.

6 Prosocial Issues

"Prosocial" has now become the accepted shorthand for designating television programming that is seen as having positive social content" (Lee, 1988, p.238). Most literature on the effects of the mass media focuses on anti-social, negative aspects. Simultaneously with these may occur pro-social positive influences. As Messenger Davies (1989) has argued, its a pity so little attention has been given to the nicer face of television. However a few reviews exist - (Lee 1988; Rushton 1982; Johnston and Ettema 1986). In terms of formal studies of television content there are very few which have attempted to assess the amount of co-operation, friendliness sharing etc despite numerous studies on violence and aggression.

The first attempt to measure prosocial behaviours appears to have been Liebert and Poulos (1975) and Poulos, Harvey and Liebert (1976) followed by Greenberg et al's (1980) large study: *Life on Television*. Liebert and Poulos analysed 300 prime time, afternoon and cartoon programmes broadcast on American television in 1974. They found averages of 11 altruistic acts and 6 sympathetic behaviours per hour. Control of aggressive impulses and resistance to temptation were less frequent at less than one per hour. In a later study of Saturday morning children's television, Poulos et al (1976) report a similar rate of 13 altruistic acts and 5 sympathetic responses per hour. Greenberg et al (1980) over a 3 year period from 1975 through to 1978 found 20 acts of altruism per hour. In addition "explaining the feelings of self and others" occurred at a rate of 22 acts per hour. (Greenberg also measured aggression very generously and reports a rate of 14 acts per hour. The more conventional measure of violence produces a rate between 5 and 8 acts per hour).

More recently Lee (1988) has summarised the results of 4 weeks network prime time television entertainment programming during 1985-86 which gave 235 programmes. Prosocial behaviours observed totalled 1,035 incidents. Over one third of these were sympathy/empathy (37%) followed by 'showing affection' (15%). The sub-categories of sharing, co-operation and altruism add up to 21% of all prosocial behaviours followed by use of reasoning (15%), resistance to temptation (5%) and showing remorse (5%). Unfortunately Lee does not report an overall rate per hour but mentions prosocial behaviour is most common in situation comedies and drama at 5 incidents per hour than in action adventure programmes (3 per hour).

A much smaller study by Selnow (1986) on 66 prime time "scripted series" examined problem resolution. Confrontational approaches were adopted in nearly half (43%) of situations (this included assertive behaviour, 25%; aggression, 16%; verbal aggression, 2%). Communicative (mutual agreement) types occurred in 18.5% of problems followed passive, helping, concession and various other non-confrontational approaches.

Unfortunately no attempt has been made to study prosocial behaviour on British television. Clearly focussing on aggression and violence disguises the oppositional messages which occur (Newcomb and Hirsch 1984). Moreover there are no studies of how oppositional messages may be processed by the audience. There have been a large number of studies dealing with prosocial issues but these have concentrated on the effects of consciously prosocial programmes such as *Seasame Street, Freestyle* and *Mister Roger's Neighbourhood.*

Hearold (1986) argued that prosocial television has a more powerful influence to increase prosocial behaviour than anti-social/violent programmes seem to have in encouraging aggression. However this conclusion is based on a statistical averaging of all available studies (called Meta analysis). Most of the research in this field has used young children as subjects in experiments where children may be easily led to play what game they think the experimenter wants. Thus the generalisability of most experiments to natural settings will be very limited. Evaluations of *Freestyle*

23

(Johnson and Ettema 1980) indicate some of the problems. Children viewing the programme at school showed consistent attitude change; children viewing at home recorded very few changes (only among the heaviest viewers on one measure out of 20). Similar conclusions must be drawn about *Sesame Street*. It is difficult not to share the enthusiasm of those who designed and evaluated *Sesame Street*. The goal of this programme was to help the education of disadvantaged children - to reach those parts that schools apparently could not teach. However the effects of viewing the programme are difficult to assess. The largest effects found were due to parental encouragement but there was no difference between heavy viewers who were encouraged and light viewers who were encouraged. Moreover advantaged groups tended to gain more from the series than disadvantaged children (Cook et al 1975, Salomon 1976).

Mister Roger's Neighbourhood seemed to encourage imaginative play according to a well designed study by Singer and Singer (1976). "However the effect was contingent on the presence of a 'mediator' who interpreted events in the programme and directed children's attention to relevant program cues." (Feshbach 1988, p.264)... ..."television content may have to be reinforced by other socialising influences to sustain its impact" (Feshbach 1988, p.265). Although most of the published literature has sought to demonstrate the value of prosocial television, Coates et al (1976) found that pre-school children who had viewed *Sesame Street* and *Mister Roger's Neighbourhood* became more aggressive: low aggressive children showed an almost threefold increase over their baseline aggression scores! If this effect is reliable (as Singer and Singer, 1981, 1986 suggest it is) then more attention needs to be given to the processes operating between television and the child or rather - between the child and television.

7   Sex and Violence

Although sex and violence are often linked in public debate sexual violence is treated quite separately from sex or violence in the research literature. Very little research evidence exists on the portrayal of sexual behaviour and consists of rather mechanical content analyses of the amount of kissing and hugging on television carried out in America (Franzblan et al 1977; Sprafkin et al 1981 and Greenberg 1981). No research data seems to exist on the effects of such portrayals. Sexual violence has long been researched but focuses on the kind of pornography which is not broadcast at least in Britain. Only in the case of violence is there a comprehensive literature on television content and its possible effects.

The violence content of television has been recently measured by Cumberbatch et al (1987) and reviewed by Cumberbatch et al (1988) describing patterns in the UK and elsewhere. In this comparison Britain appears to have less violence than any other country for which comparable data exists. At 2.5 violent acts per hour British viewers are exposed to less than half the amount of violence than viewers in Holland, New Zealand, Australia, Germany, Japan or the United States. The patterns of violence evident reveal similarities between countries - especially America and Britain. For example graphic detail is largely absent. However the available information on the different kinds of violence presented in different contexts has not fed in to effects research.

Literature on the effects of television violence is considerable but rarely is any discrimination made about the kinds of scenes shown or the types of programmes used. Most research conclusions have been that some link exists between media violence and viewers' aggression but such conclusions have been regularly challenged. Such challenges arise from different quarters but need to be understood in the context of media research as a whole.

Effects research in context

The history of mass communication research is conspicuously lacking in any clear evidence on the precise influence of the mass media. Theories abound, examples multiply, but convincing facts that specific media content is reliably associated with particular effects have proved quite elusive. As we have seen, there is a certain consistency in the research over this. Nevertheless within particular problem areas, strong arguments are regularly offered for powerful effects. Only in the case of violence does there seem any substantial research evidence offered to support popular concerns. This research evidence however remains quite controversial. Much of the controversy revolves around the methodologies used and interpretations which are possible.

At this stage perhaps the central issue to address is one of policy implications. If for the moment we accept that the evidence does indeed support a link between violence on television and aggression in society - what is the link? What kind of violence should broadcasters reduce? Here a rather serious problem arises. A disturbing number of studies point to the process of generalised arousal as the key elements - in other words any programme which is arousing may produce short-term effects such as increased aggressivity. In a careful re-analysis of 20 field experiments using violent media fare and control films, Gadow and Sprafkin (1989) conclude that most often it is the 'control' programmes which are most problematical:

> The fact that children react to many different types of television programs has at least two important implications. First, encouraging children to watch 'wholesome' television is not the solution to ameliorating conduct problems and would appear on the basis of the available evidence to be counter

25

productive. Second efforts to teach children about television, particularly curicula designed to make them less reactive to its content, should be broadly based. In other words, they should address a variety of topics (eg. special effects, reality-v-fantasy) and program contents (ie. aggressive and non-aggressive shows). (Gadow and Sprafkin 1989, p.9)

It is unfortunate that so much research has taken such a narrow focus on the issues that this finding has escaped detection until now. Even worse researchers have not directed attention to the specific policy questions broadcasters ask. Dorr (1988) for example lists 22 multipart questions she has been asked by broadcasters such as "is it better if the aggression is shown explicitly or more implicitly? Does it matter why characters aggress?" and so on. Unhappily social scientists attempting to answer these questions can only be intuitive, extrapolating dangerously from unreliable data. But the questions remain as serious ones. Far more attention needs to be given to the dilemma that broadcasters face. Research on this has hardly begun (Dorr 1988; Harding 1988; Katz 1988; Abel 1988; Lesyna & Phillips 1989).

It is difficult to find much research evidence within the mass communications literature which can be fed directly into policy documents. This isn't because social scientists are inevitably circumspect. There are plenty of "one armed" researchers around after (Harry Truman who asked for a one armed lawyer - because laywers always say "well, on the one hand, it's this, and on the other hand, it's that). The problem lies intrinsically with the search for media effects. Feshbach (1988) suggests "It can be argued that the concern with definitive research findings has served to obfuscate and impede the implementation of meaningful social policy in the child-television arena" (Feshbach 1988, p.200).

Essentially similar conclusions were reached over three decades ago in mass communications. What seems long overdue is a new research agenda which will focus both on broadcasters and the viewing public whose various concerns are poorly represented by our existing knowledge. Perhaps its time for researchers at least to switch their television sets off and get down to some useful work.

KEY REFERENCES

ALLEN, C. (1965) 'Photographing the TV audience' *Journal of Advertising Research* 5, p.2-8.

ALVARADO, M., GUTCH, R. & WOLLEN, T. (1987) *Learning the Media - An Introduction to Media Teaching* London, Macmillan.

ANWAR, M. & SHANG, A. (1982) *Television in a multi-racial society*. London, Commission for Racial Equality.

BAKER, R.K. & BALL, S. (1969) *Mass Media and Violence*. Washington DC; US Govt. Printing Office.

BALL, S, PALMER, P. & MILLWARD, E. (1986) 'Television and its educational impact' in Bryant & Zillman (1986) p.129-142.

BARCUS, E.G. (1983) *Images of Life on Children's Television*. New York, Praeger.

BARWISE, P. & EHRENBERG, A. (1989) *Television and its audience* London, Sage.

BEENTJES, J.W.J. & VAN DER VOORT, T.H.A. (1988) 'Television's impact on children's reading skills: a review of research' *Reading Research Quarterly* 23 (4), p.389-413.

BRETE, D.J. & CANTOR, J. (1988) 'The portrayal of men and women in US television commercials: a recent content analysis and trends over 15 years' *Sex Roles*, 18 (9-10), p.595-609.

BRODY, S. (1976) *Screen Violence and Film Censorship* London, HMSO.

BROWN, B. (1989) *Studying Media Audiences from an Ethnographic Perspective*. *Report to the Broadcasting Standards Council* Aston University, Birmingham.

BRYANT, J. & ZILLMAN, D. (eds) (1986) *Perspectives on Media Effects* Hillsdale, N.J., USA: L. Erlbaum.

CUMBERBATCH, G. (1988) 'Media and racism' in E. Cashmore (ed) *Dictionary of Race and Ethnic Relations* London Routledge, p.184-186.

CUMBERBATCH, G., HARDY, G. & LEE, M. (1987) *The portrayal of violence on British Television* London, BBC.

CUMBERBATCH, G., JONES, I. & LEE, M. (1988) 'Measuring violence on television' *Current Psychology Research and Reviews* 7 (1), p.10-25.

CUMBERBATCH, G., LEE, M., GRICE, Y., WATSON T. & WOON, J. (forthcoming) *Images of Disablement* London, Broadcasting Research Unit.

DAIL, P.W. (1988) 'Prime-time television portrayals of older adults in the context of family life' *The Gerontologist* 28 (5) p.700-706.

DEFLEUR, M & BALL-ROKEACH, S. (1989) *Theories of Mass Communications* New York Longman.

DOCHERTY, D., MORRISON, D. & TRACEY, M. (1986) 'Who goes to the cinema?' *Sight and Sound* 55, p.81-85.
 - (1987) *The Last Picture Show? Britain's Changing Film Audience* London, BFI

DORR, A. (1988) 'When social scientists cooperate with Broadcasting' *Applied Social Psychology Annual* 8 p.285-303.

DUNKLEY, C. (1985) *Television Today and Tomorrow - Wall to Wall Dallas?* Harmondsworth, , Penguin.

DURKIN, K. (1985) *Television, Sex Roles and Children* Milton Keynes, Open University Press.

EQUAL OPPORTUNITIES COMMISSION (1988) *Women and Men in Britain: A Research Profile* London, HMSO.

FESHBACH, S. (1988) 'Television research and social policy' *Applied Social Psychology Annual* 8, 11 p.198-214.

GADOW, K.D. & SPRAFKIN, J. (1989) 'Field experiments of television violence' *Pediatrics 83*, March (in press).

GREENBERG, B.S. (1980) *Life on Television* Norwood, NJ, Ablex Publishing.

GREENBERG, B.S.(1986) 'Minorities and the mass media' in J. Bryant & D Zillman (eds) *Perspectives on Media Effects* Hillsdale NJ, L. Erlbaum, p.165-188.

GUNTER, B. & SVENNEVIG, M. (1987) *Behind and in Front of the Screen* London, John Libbey.

HANSEN, A. (1988a) Young People, Television and Alcohol. Leicester, Centre for Mass Communications Research.
 - (1988b)*The Portrayal of Alcohol In Popular Television Series* Leicester, UK: Centre for Mass Communications Research.

HARDING, P.A. (1988) 'Social science research and media policy issues' *Applied Social Psychology Annual* 8, p.304-310.

HARTMANN, P. & HUSBAND, C. (1974) *Racism and the Mass Media* London, Davis-Poynter.

HEAROLD, S. (1986) 'A synthesis of 1043 effects of television on social behaviour' in G. Comstock (ed) *Public Communications and Behavior* Vol. 1 New York, Academic Press.

HIMMELWEIT, H.T., OPPENHEIM, A.N. & VINCE, P. (1958) *Television and the Child* London, Oxford University Press.

JOHNSON, J. & ETTEMA, J. (1982) *Positive Images: Breaking Stereotypes with Childrens Television* Beverly Hills, CA, Sage.

JOHNSON, J. & ETTEMA, J. (1986) 'Using television to best advantage: research for prosocial television' *Applied Social Psychology Annual* 8, p.143-164.

JOWELL, R., WITHERSPOON, S. & BROOK, L. (1988) *British Social Attitudes* Aldershot, Gower.

KARPF, A. (1988) *Doctoring the Media.* London, Routledge.

KATZ, E. (1988) 'On conceptualising media effects' *Applied Social Psychology Annual* 8, 361-374.

KLAPPER, J. (1960) *The Effects of Mass Communication* New York: Free Press.

LAMBERT, J., LASLETT, P. & CLAY, H. (1984) *The Image of the elderly on TV* Cambridge, U3A.

LARGE, M. (1980) *Who's Bringing Them Up?* Gloucester, Alan Sutton Publishing.

LAZARSFELD, P.F., BERELSON, B. & GAUDET, H. (1944) *The People's Choice* New York: Duell.

LEE, B. (1988) 'Prosocial content on prime-time television' *Applied Social Psychology Annual* 8, 238-246.

LESYNA, K. & PHILLIPS, D.P. (1989) 'Suicide and the Media: Research and Policy Implications' in R. Diekstra. *The World Health Organization for Preventive Strategies on Suicide: A WHO State of the Art Publication.*

LIEBERT, R.M. & SPRAFKIN, J. (1988) *The Early Window* New York: Pergamon.

LINDOLF, T.R. (1986) *Natural Audiences: Qualitative Research on Media Uses and Effects* Norwood, NJ, Ablex.

LIVINGSTONE, S & GREEN, G. (1986) 'Television advertisements and the portrayal of gender' *British Journal of Social Psychology* 25 p.149-154.

LOWERY, S. & DEFLEUR, M.L. (1983) *Milestones in Mass Communications Research: Media Effects* New York: Longman.

NEUMAN, S.B. (1988) 'The displacement effect: assessing the relation between television viewing and reading performance' *Reading Research Quarterly* 23 (4), p.414-440.

NEWCOMB, H. & HIRSCH, P. (1984) 'Television as a cultural forum' in W. Rowland & B. Watkins (eds) *Interpreting Television: Current Research Perspectives* Newbury Park, California, Sage, p.58-73.

MAHAJAN, V. & PETERSON, R.A. (1985) *Models for Innovation Diffusion* Beverly Hills, California, Sage.

MANDER, J. (1980) *Four Arguments for the Elimination of Television* Brighton, Harvester Press.

McCAULEY & THANGAVELU, K. (1988) 'Sex stereotyping of occupations in relation to television representations and census facts' *Basic and Applied Social Psychology* 9 (3) p.197-212.

McQUAIL, D. (1987) *Mass Communication Theory* London, Sage.

MESSENGER DAVIES, M. (1989) *Television is Good for Your Kids* London, Hilary Shipman.

PALMER, E.L. (1989) *Television and America's Children: a crisis of neglect* New York, Oxford University Press.

PALMER, P. (1986) *The Lively Audience* London Allen & Unwin.

PEARL, D., BOUTHILET, L. & LAZAR, J. (eds) (1982) *Television and Behavior: Ten Years of Scientific Progress* Rockville, Maryland, N.I.M.H.

POINDEXTER, P.M. & STROMAN, C.A. (1981) 'Blacks and television: a review of the research literature' *Journal of Broadcasting* 25 p.103-122.

POSTMAN, N. (1983) *The Disappearance of Childhood* London, WH Allen.

ROGERS, E.M. (1983) *Diffusion of Innovations* New York, Macmillan.

ROSENGREN, K.E., WERNER, L.A. & PALMGREEN, P. (eds) (1985) *Media Gratifications Research: Current Perspectives* Newbury Park, CA, Sage.

RUSHTON, J.P. (1982) 'Television and prosocial behavior' in Pearl, Bouthilet & Lazar (1982) p.248-258.

SCHRAMM, W., LYLE, J. & PARKER, E.B. (1961) *Television in the Lives of Our Children* Stanford, CA, Stanford University Press.

SCOTT, R.N. (1975) *Sex Role Stereotyping in Women's Magazine Advertisements* Aston University, Ph.D. Thesis.

SHULMAN, M. (1973) *The Ravenous Eye* London, Cornet Books.

SIGNORIELLI, N. (1985a) *Role Portrayal and Stereotyping on Television* Westport, Conn, Greenwood Press.

- (1985b) 'The demography of the television world' in Melischek, K.E., Rosengren, J. & Stappers, J. (eds) *Cultural Indicators* Vienna, Austrian Academy of Sciences.

SIGNORIELLI, N. & GERBNER, G. (1988) *Violence and Terror in the Mass Media* New York, Greenwood.

SINGER, D.C. (1982) 'Television and the developing imagination of the child'. in Pearl, Bouthilet & Lazar, p.39-52.

SINGER, J.L. & SINGER, D.G. (1986) 'Family experiences and television viewing as predictors of children's imagination, restlessness and aggression' *Journal of Social Issues* 42 (3) pp.107-124.

SILVERSTONE, R. (1989) 'Let us return to the murmurings of everday practices'*Theory Culture and Society* 6, p.77-94.

SOLOMON, D.S. (1982) 'Health campaigns on television'. In Pearl, Bouthilet and Lazar, pp.308-321.

SVENNEVIG, M. & WYNBERG, B. (1986) 'Viewing is viewing is viewing or is it?' *Admap* (May) 11 pp.267-274.

TAYLOR, L. & MULLAN, B. (1986) *Uninvited Guests: the intimate secrets of television and radio* London, Chatto and Windus.

WARTELLA, E. (1988) 'The public context of debates about television and children' *Applied Social Psychology Annual* 8 pp.59-68.

WARTELLA, E. & REEVES, B. (1985) 'Historical trends in research on children and the media: 1900-1960' *Journal of Communication* 35, pp.118-133.

WARZAK, W.J. et al (1988) 'An analysis of televised presentations of disability' *Rehabilitation Psychology* 33 (2) pp.105-112.

WERNER, J.S. & TANKARD, J.W. (1988) *Communication Theories* New York: Longman.

WINN, M. (1977, 1985) *The Plug-in Drug* New York, Viking Press.

WINNICK, C. (1988) 'The functions of television: life without the Big Box' *Applied Social Psychology Annual* 8 217-237.

WOBER, M. & GUNTER, B. (1988) *Television and Social Control* Aldershot, Avebury.

II: VIOLENCE AND THE MASS MEDIA: The Research Evidence

Dr Guy Cumberbatch

Introduction

There is little doubt that people are concerned about crime and violence. Public opinion polls reliably place these issues among the top ones for government action (NORC, 1980; Heath, Jowell and Curtice, 1985). Moreover, as a cause for concern, crime is rated higher than any other issue except unemployment in America, Britain, Italy and Holland (see Watkins and Worcester, 1986). And yet crime and violence remain remarkably rare personal experiences for the vast majority of the public. Thus according to the most reliable estimates, most of us can enjoy at least a few decades of a crime free existence. A tiny minority of us will become criminals, and a few more will be the victims of crime but even then the offences are likely to be fairly trivial (see Hough & Mayhew 1985; Walmsley, 1986). In the meantime however, secondary experiences of serious crime and violence will be a daily phenomenon. Depending on the newspapers read, the radio stations listened to and the television programmes watched, the average person's secondary experiences of crime and violence might well run to around 7,000 acts per annum in the UK and more in the other countries like the USA (estimated from Cumberbatch and Beardsworth, 1976; Cumberbatch, Jones and Lee, 1988).

Could it be, therefore, that the mass media create public concern about crime and violence? Early research seemed to support this hypothesis strongly. For example, Gerbner demonstrated a pleasing positive correlation between the amount of television viewing and 'fear of victimisation' (Gerbner, Gross, Eleey, Jackson-Beeck, Jeffries-Fox and Signorielli, 1977, 1978). This made sense - obviously those exposed to a lot of television would see much that suggested a dangerous world. The social consequences of an increased fear of crime are open to various interpretations but recent evidence suggests it may be part of an escalating loop where fear of crime constrains social behaviour which itself further increases fear of crime (Liska, Sanchiro and Reed, 1988). Although not undisputed (Hughes, 1980; Hirsch, 1980, 1981a, 1981b) the essential findings of Gerbner et al were replicated in a number of studies (for

31

example, Bryant, Carvether and Brown, 1981; Hawkins and Pingree, 1980; Williams, Zabrack and Joy, 1982; Morgan, 1983). But then Gunter and Wober challenged this simple hypothesis with a more careful analysis of the problem (Wober and Gunter 1982, Gunter and Wober 1983). Instead of assuming what viewers would watch if they were heavy viewers of television they asked subjects to keep diaries of what they watched. The diaries were used to correlate viewing with measures covered in the earlier studies and various additional measures, including personality attributes such as locus of control (the belief that one can control one's own destiny). When locus of control was held constant, the relationship between amounts of viewing and fear of victimisation disappeared. In other words, personality may explain the link between television viewing and fear of crime: those people who feel that what happens to them is not under their control tend to watch a lot of television and also tend to be afraid of being victimised by criminals (Gunter, 1987; Wober and Gunter, 1988).

Over the years the interesting idea of Gerbner's that television (because of its crime and violence) cultivates a fear of crime has been shown to be inadequate. Viewers may be quite discriminating in their perceptions of crime on television and in society (Tamborini et al. 1984). Perceptions of how much crime there is may not be necessarily related to fear of crime (Tyler and Cook, 1984), while Mendelsohn concluded that if "the media cultivate anything, they appear to cultivate crime prevention competence among such publics - not hysteria" (Mendelsohn, 1983, p7). All in all, few empirical studies lend full support to the original Gerbner hypothesis, while there are many failures to replicate (Killias, 1983; Stroman and Settger, 1985; Wober and Gunter, 1982, 1988; Piepe, Crouch and Emerson, 1977).

The ubiquity of crime and violence in the mass media has stimulated a whole host of debates about how far the media may encourage anxieties, shape attitudes, define values or excite behaviour in the public. Not surprisingly the most persistent concern has been that mass media violence causes violence in society. Indeed arguably this has been the most researched question in mass communications, accounting for probably well over a thousand research publications spanning psychology, psychiatry and sociology (for example, NIMH, 1982).

The pattern of conclusions to this research seems fairly clear cut. Andison's (1977) calculation that 77% of the studies claim that media violence causes violence in real life probably still holds true (for example, Hearold, 1986; Huesmann and Malamuth, 1986; Liebert and Sprafkin, 1988). Nevertheless, in most respects the research has been quite inadequate and on close examination simply does not concur in the way most reviews argue. In recent years there have been a number of critical reviews challenging the consensus view on this vexed issue of television violence (for example, Coughlin, 1985; Freedman, 1984, 1986, 1988; McGuire, 1986; Gadow & Sprafkin, 1989). It would be useful therefore to examine some of the key studies a little more closely before venturing to overview the reasons for so much disagreement in this field.

As a general issue media violence has provoked essentially similar concerns about its potential harmful effects with the introduction of each new medium: the cinema, radio, comic books and television (Howitt and Cumberbatch, 1975; Wartella & Reeves 1985). In the history of mass communications research, some of the early studies are of great interest - notably those carried out for the Payne Fund on the relationship between the movies and delinquency (for example, Cressey and Thrasher, 1933; Shuttleworth and May, 1933). However, a combination of events in the 1960's stimulated a whole host of research on the effects of television. Notable in the early 1960's was the development of laboratory based research and this new research tradition provides a convenient starting point for this review.

Laboratory Research

The most frequently cited studies in this field are those initiated by two psychologists: Albert Bandura at Stanford University and Leonard Berkowitz at the University of Wisconsin. Both researchers focused on film mediated aggression rather than crime per se. Neither were stimulated by applied psychological considerations but began their work in a theoretical context and almost accidentally addressed media related issues.

Albert Bandura's first study, which noted the imitation of aggression in pre-school children (Bandura and Huston, 1961) was designed to examine whether the attractiveness of a teacher influenced learning. However, one of the acts which the 'teacher' committed was an aggressive one and this was readily imitated, regardless of the 'nurturant' quality, or otherwise, of the teacher. From this initial observation Bandura rapidly focused on imitative aggression, comparing filmed models with live models (see for example, Bandura, Ross and Ross, 1961, 1963). As Bandura noted "since the studies are mainly concerned with issues of learning, the aggressive acts modelled are those that are rarely, if ever, displayed by children who have had no exposure to the modelled performances" (Bandura, 1973, p72). The object of the aggression was a large knockdown plastic clown (called a Bobo or Bozo doll) which when struck violently would, due to its weighted base, bounce back up again. "In the general procedure, after addressing the figure belligerently, the model pommels it on the head with a mallet, hurls it down, sits on it and punches it on the nose repeatedly, kicks it across the room, flings it into the air, and bombards it with balls" (Bandura, 1973, p72). After exposure to the model's curious antics, children are frustrated by showing them some attractive toys they are invited to admire but told they may not play with. Finally, children are led to a room containing similar objects to the ones the model had used and ostensibly left alone to play. In reality the children are observed through

33

one way mirrors and their aggressive behaviour monitored. Perhaps not surprisingly most children (up to 88%) readily imitate the models and are able to reproduce more than 70% of the responses observed immediately after exposure and even 8 months later may still retain 40% of them (see for example, Hicks, 1968).

Before considering the value of this style of research for our understanding of media effects, it is worth summarising the paradigm adopted by Leonard Berkowitz, whose work was centrally concerned with learning theory perspectives on aggression as pioneered by psychologists at Yale (for example, Dollard, Doob, Miller, Mowrer and Sears, 1939). His use of film material was simply an extension of the techniques used to investigate the inhibition or catharsis of hostility (see for example, Berkowitz, 1962). Feshbach (1955, 1961) had argued that fantasy behaviour performed a drive-reducing (cathartic) function. Those who saw an aggressive film were less aggressive than those who had not. Berkowitz was unconvinced by this evidence and demonstrated (Berkowitz and Rawlings, 1963) that any reduction in aggression from watching an aggressive film is more likely to be due to the film heightening a subject's anxiety about his own display of aggression rather than the aggression becoming vicariously discharged due to the film. The general procedure adopted by Berkowitz involved six groups of subjects (university students) who first of all received an intelligence test. Half of the groups were angered by an experimenter (who insulted the intellectual competence of the subjects) while the other hand were treated in a neutral fashion. Following this, half of the groups saw the control film (about canal boats in England) whilst the other half saw a seven minute film clip of the prize fight taken from *Champion* starring Kirk Douglas. One experimental group was informed that the aggression against Kirk Douglas in the film was "justified" (in order to reduce subjects' aggression anxiety) while the other group were told that it was not (in order to increase their aggression anxiety). Finally a second experimenter invited subjects to complete a questionnaire on what they thought of the experimenter to send to his boss.

The results indicated that those angered by the experimenter made more adverse comments about him than those treated neutrally. In the angered groups those who had been instructed that the aggression in the film was justified made significantly more aggressive responses than the control film group or the "unjustified aggression" film group. The films did not have any differential effects on the non-angered groups. Thus, Berkowitz concluded that "media aggression depicted as being justified has the greatest probability of leading to aggression when the audience is already angry" (Berkowitz, 1962, p243).

Although studies from these two different styles of research remain distinctive they have often been lumped together as showing that the "conclusions from all this work must be that viewing violence increases the chances of aggression occurring" (for example, Eysenck and Nias, 1978, p160-1). However, such a conclusion glosses

34

over some important distinctions and contradictions, as well as various methodological problems.

First of all, in the case of Bandura's research, there must be little doubt that children can learn by 'observational' or 'social' learning. This is clearly part and parcel of the way children become socialised. However, despite continuing research demonstrating such modelling behaviour (for example, McHan, 1985) there is a growing dissatisfaction with the ecological validity of the laboratory experiment: children do not typically imitate all that they see or even attempt to do so. There is a quite fundamental discrepancy between the high incidence of imitation in Bandura's results and what children typically do after watching television (play normally, have their tea and so on). Undoubtedly, the novelty of the Bobo doll was a crucial factor. Kniveton and Stephenson (1970) found that children who were unfamiliar with the doll imitated 5 times more than did children with previous exposure to it. Nobel (1975) comments "in my own studies, where children watch media violence in small groups I have rarely found more than 5 per cent imitation after viewing" (Noble, 1975, p134). Milgram and Shotland (1973) reported a series of eight major field experiments on the effects of modelled behaviour in the mass media. Despite the fact that these studies involved sample sizes of, at times, millions, there was no evidence that television models were imitated. On the other hand, Eysenck and Nias (1978), and Liebert, Neale and Davidson (1973) both cite many popular accounts of 'waves of violence' following media portrayals of particular acts. Bomb hoaxes, suicides and sundry other aggressive acts are attributed to television's power to encourage 'copycat' behaviour. However much of this evidence is anecdotal and ignores the role of news values in reporting such phenomena; for example, a wave of media reports of dogs savaging children owes more to the newsworthiness of such stories increasing after the first report than on imitative behaviour in the canine species.

It is worth noting that the findings reported by Phillips (Phillips, 1982, 1983; Phillips and Hensley, 1984; Phillips, 1986; Lesyna & Phillips, 1989) on the impact of well publicised media stories on fatal antisocial behaviour. He argued for example that daily suicides increase significantly after highly publicised suicide stories appear on television. Unfortunately this interesting approach has now produced many contradictory results (Berman, 1988; Kessler and Stipp, 1984; Kessler, Downey, Milavsky and Stipp, 1988; Messner, 1986; Baron and Reiss, 1985; Phillips and Carstensen, 1986; Gould and Shaffer, 1986; Pratt, 1987; Phillips and Paight, 1987). Moreover interpretation of this phenomenon is complicated by social processes influencing the labelling and reporting of these fatalities. Back to Bandura. As Hartley (1964) noted, Bandura:

> ...suggests that behavior towards inanimate objects like toys, is equated with social behavior, a suggestion which is not generally supported in the literature.

> In fact the bulk of the literature supports an opposite view, that children will express toward inanimate objects feelings that they will not dare to show openly toward other persons. (Hartley 1964 p 19)

It would seem much closer to what ethologists describe as "rough and tumble play" (Blurton-Jones, 1976; Smith, 1974) than aggression as usually understood. As Patterson, Littman and Bricker (1967) pointed out children who have never seen Bandura's films will attack a Bozo doll by hitting it on the head with a mallet if a mallet and a doll are provided!

A related issue is a more fundamental one for experimental research. Even if Bandura's measures of aggression were shown to have a convincing validity, would this hold for imitative aggression? For example an intelligence test might have some concurrent validity (for example in predicting students' exam marks) but if as an experimental treatment subjects were shown how to perform well on the test (say by an illustration in a film), would a post treatment intelligence test have much validity as a measure of intelligence? Those who did well on the test after seeing the film might not be the most intelligent. This unlikely experiment is in fact rather akin to Bandura's paradigm and highlights the serious weakness in validity criteria. As conventionally defined, these cover the static validity of dependent measures such as showing those who score highest on an intelligence test do best in exams rather than what might be termed the "dynamic validity" necessary to survive experimental treatments or indeed measure almost any kind of change over time.

Although there are numerous other methodological issues which should be raised about this research, perhaps the final points may be developed by noting the contradictions between the results of Bandura's research and those obtained by Berkowitz. For example, Berkowitz found only generalised aggression (subjects did not imitate the film) while Bandura found only imitative aggression (subjects did not generalise, Howitt, 1972). The idea of university students aggressing against Bobo dolls, acting out the film script with dramatic imitative renderings of "whack him!", "sock it" and so on, may seem a trifle absurd but illustrates an important distinction Bandura himself made between learning and performance. We all may learn how to rape, rob or murder from what we see in films or on television but the barriers to our performing these acts in everyday life are more motivational than knowledge-based. Similarly, the barriers to helping behaviour are more likely to be found in motivation or opportunity cost than in any absence of a behavioural repertoire of how to help (for example, Piliavin, Dovidion, Gaerntner and Clark, 1981). The contradictions between Bandura's results and those of Berkowitz may be due to the different populations studied or to the different films used. However, they may also be due to the different "demand characteristics" of the experiments which define the role subjects are expected to play, and if this is the explanation then the relevance of the studies to mass media effects in the real world must be seriously questioned. Noble, for example, quotes one shrewd four-year old who, on arriving at the laboratory for a modelling experiment was heard to observe to her mother "look Mummy, there's the doll we have to hit!" (Noble, 1975, p134). As Freedman (1986) observes, merely showing an aggressive film may imply the experimenter expects or even desires aggressive responses. Certainly Borden (1975) found aggressive responses were lower when female observers were present and increased if observers appeared to have aggressive values.

The idea that experiments have their own imperative or "demand characteristics" was put forward by Orne in the early 1960's to explain some disturbing evidence that subjects may not behave in a neutral or even normal fashion in psychology experiments (see for example, Adair, 1973; Friedman, 1967; Orne, 1969; Orne and Holland, 1968, Westland, 1978). The evidence that laboratory experiments on the effects of the mass media are flawed by demand characteristics is far from conclusive but sufficient to provide some grounds for concern. First of all, the experiments are very contrived procedures, even for the nursery school children in Bandura's studies. However, those of Berkowitz are remarkably so. Later experiments became yet more contrived and especially so since students generally earned "credits" for participating which counted toward their psychology degrees. Thus, Berkowitz and Geen (1967), hypothesised that when given the opportunity to aggress, subjects would do so more strongly if the victims were linked with the aggressive film in some way. Their experiment involved the experimenter being introduced as either "Kirk" who was a boxer or "Bob" who wasn't. After seeing the Kirk Douglas film sequence (where Kirk plays the role of a boxer) subjects by a happy coincidence were allowed to give electric shocks to the experimenter in a learning task. Subjects receiving the "name mediated" treatment produced the most aggressive responses (cf Berkowitz and Geen, 1966). Unfortunately, the effects of subject sophistication where those taking part guess the experimenter's hypothesis seems to have produced a mixed bag of results. Sometimes they appear to comply and in other studies lean over backwards not to do so (for example, Page and Scheidt, 1971; Shuck and Pisor, 1974, Berkowitz, 1971).

Quite apart from the problem of demand characteristics, many of the effects noted are probably more economically interpreted in terms of a state of physiological arousal than a state of aggression as such. Direct evidence comes from Zillman and Johnson (1973) who added an additional control condition of no film to compare with the effects of seeing a violent film clip (from *The Wild Bunch*) and with seeing a neutral film clip (*Marco Polo's Travels*). Physiological measures indicated that the neutral film depressed arousal relative to the no-film condition. This explained the results of the aggression measure (willingness of subjects to deliver electric shocks). Here there was no difference between the violent film and the no-film condition, both of which produced more aggression than the neutral film.

37

Further support for this idea that arousal rather than aggression is the key element is provided by Tannenbaum (Tannenbaum, 1971; Tannenbaum and Zillman, 1975). For example, humorous films produced more aggression than control films, but aggressive films were quite as effective in increasing humorous responses to humorous material. Similarly non-aggressive erotic film material increased rewarding behaviour where the learning task required this rather than punishment. Mueller, Donnerstein and Hallam (1983) reported a 50% increase in pro social behaviour following exposure to a violent programme. Zillman went on to develop a more comprehensive "excitation-transfer theory" to account for these and various related findings (Zillman, 1978, 1979, 1982) and later extended this to cover the gratifications audiences may enjoy from various media exposure (for example, Zillman and Bryant, 1986) which will be discussed later.

In this context the work of Huston-Stein et al (1981) is worth mentioning - they found that youngsters were as attentive to cartoons high in action but low in violence as they were to violent cartoons but showed just as much aggression in a subsequent free play situation as they did to a high action high violence programme. Similar conclusions were reached by Linne (1976).

The most cited of recent research has focused on the effects of aggressive pornographic material on aggressive behaviour. Thus a series of experiments by Donnerstein and Berkowitz (1981) continued the tradition of deceiving college students that they were taking part in an experiment on learning (using electric shock), whereas in reality anger arousal and the effects of filmed material were being evaluated (see also Malamuth and Donnerstein, 1984; Donnerstein, Linz and Penrod, 1987). With angered subjects none of the sexual films used affected levels of aggression against another male but when male subjects were allowed to aggress against a female, the pornographic films significantly increased the shock intensity delivered. In the case of non-angered subjects the only interesting result was due to the film condition, which depicted a woman enjoying sexual violence. Under this condition subjects were nearly as aggressive towards a female victim as were angered men towards male victims. While it is tempting to deal with this literature in more detail it is covered in the next chapter. Suffice it to say that the research conclusions provoked a vitriolic debate in two major journals: *The American Psychologist*, 1987, and *Journal of Communication*, 1987, primarily about the interpretation of laboratory research.

Within the mass communications literature there exists a fairly rigid scepticism about laboratory based research (for example, Brown, 1970; McQuail, 1969, 1987). However, close analysis of the problems such as given above is almost completely absent, thus leading to a suspicion that most reviewers are simply dismissive of methodologies which are not germane to their own experience. It is hoped that the attention given here to the methodological problems of experiments will lead to both a more informed debate and provide a salutary lesson for experimental researchers. Greater ecological validity in experiments, more thoughtful and thorough designs are all possible (and certainly long overdue), in order to deal satisfactorily with the vexed issue of mass media effects.

By way of conclusion to this section, we may observe that laboratory experiments do not adequately address the problem of whether or not mass media violence causes violence in society. The ecological aspects of crime and of media use have not been properly acknowledged in laboratory studies. Broadcasters who are concerned about whether their programmes are harmful would find it very difficult to use the experimental data to make specific policy decisions and for the most part may view such research with an incredulity shared by an increasing number of academic researchers.

Experimental Field Studies

At first sight field experiments attempting to manipulate the natural media diet of people in natural settings seem the most promising solution to the various criticisms of laboratory research. The first study and those that followed were a salutary reminder that field research generates its own very considerable problems and is a far from easy solution.

The first attempt to apply experimental methods to a natural setting was carried out by Feshbach and Singer (1971) in three private schools and four boys' homes. The boys were subjected to either a diet of violent television or a diet of neutral television. Some immediate problems arose. The neutral group complained bitterly about their diet and by popular request the television series *Batman* (a 'violent' programme) had to be allowed. The experiment continued for six weeks, during which houseparents and teachers recorded the boys' behaviour. In the private schools little difference was observed between the violent television group and the neutral television group. However, in the boys' homes, aggression towards peers in the violent television group was almost half that in the neutral television group. Feshbach and Singer concluded that this was evidence for catharsis - an unpopular conclusion which stimulated some critical reviews. One of the more serious methodological problems was that the observers knew which programmes the children had watched (for example, Geen and Thomas, 1986). However, some indication of the consequences of this are provided by a very similar field experiment carried out by Wells (1973) who manipulated television diets in ten residential schools. The main finding was that verbal aggression was higher in the neutral television group than in the violent television group (supporting Fechbach's notions of catharsis). However, Wells did note some causes for concern. Although there was no significant effect overall on physical aggression, boys who were above average on aggression in the violent television group became more aggressive during the experiment. This result must be seen in context as it relates to Feshbach and Singer's study. Some raters inadvertently became aware of the group to which a boy belonged. On closer analysis the effects of this was that boys were more likely to be rated as aggressive if they were known to watching violent films. Public opinion that television violence is harmful clearly may confound research endeavours investigating the question of whether it is or not.

Historically the next study worthy of note was rather different, focusing on possible imitation of a popular TV programme *Medical Center* which Milgram and Shotland (1973) edited to produce two antisocial versions and one prosocial version of the same basic story. In a large series of field experiments they found no evidence of imitative antisocial behaviour in the various audiences.

No study is perfect and in reviewing studies which support a no effects thesis of television it is tempting to list each and every problem which researchers face in this field. However persistently the methodological problems seem to produce bias in favour of effects being found. For example, Stein and Freidrich (1975a) examined the effects of aggressive, prosocial or neutral films on 3-6 year old children's free play during the four week study and for two weeks afterwards. Stein and Freidrich concluded as did Wells (above) that those who were above average on aggression at the beginning of the study tended to become more aggressive and less prosocial if they watched aggressive films. Perhaps more importantly, as Freedman (1988) noted, Stein and Friedrich did not find any overall effect of violent programmes versus neutral ones. The significant results due to high aggressive children actually showed a decline in aggression after viewing violent films but this was less than in the neutral film group while low aggression children increased aggressivity after the violent film. Unfortunately this result seems to have been due to the failure to match the groups initially on aggression - when this matching was done, the differences between groups became insignificant (Stein and Freidrich, 1975b), a fact which seems to have become forgotten in recent reviews (for example, Freidrich, Cofer and Huston, 1986).

In studies using experimental field techniques, the only important ones to conclude unreservedly that films mediate aggression have been associated with Leonard Berkowitz (Leyens, Camino, Parke & Berkowitz, 1975; Parke, Berkowitz, Leyens, West and Sebastian, 1977). In both studies, delinquent boys tended to become more aggressive during the week in which they were exposed to aggressive films every evening, compared with groups exposed to neutral films. In common with many previous studies by Berkowitz the results seem very impressive at first sight. For example, the effects of one or more violent films was to increase aggression by more than fortyfold in some groups of subjects over the baseline measures. This is curious, especially since during the film experiment the delinquents were not allowed to watch

40

television. Why should films be so dramatically more effective than television? Whatever second thoughts on the results might be, there is no escaping the serious weakness in the research. First of all, the measure of aggression was grandiosely described as a "non-hierarchical, minimally interventional, time sampling observational procedure". On closer examination this procedure would not seem capable of discriminating between a serious fight and an active game of basketball since "playful as well as malicious attacks were scored identically". Moreover, the coders responsible for the data collection were undergraduate students, who may have been aware of the experimental condition which they were monitoring, although no evidence is available on this point. However, it seems unlikely that the students were ignorant of Berkowitz's stance in this area or that they did not communicate with each other or their subjects.

Experimental field studies seem at first sight a useful approach to understanding the impact that the mass media have on society. However to date, methodological problems seriously undermine confidence that we might have had in them.

Correlational Studies

At least with correlational studies most people these days are aware that correlations may be caused by uncontrolled variables - a problem which introduced this chapter. However, correlational research showing that delinquents prefer aggressive television is all too easy to conduct. The bulk of the studies using this methodology claim a simple relationship between television violence and aggression in viewers, but one that becomes more and more elusive as the sophistication of the study increases.

The introduction of television in the 1950's stimulated a number of major studies on its potential impact. Happily the unique opportunity to carry out before and after studies was not missed either in North America or in Britain. Large scale and fairly comprehensive evaluations were conducted by Himmelweit, Oppenhmeim and Vince (1958) in Britain and by Schramm, Lyle and Parker (1961) in Canada and the United States. Although these might be better described as natural experiments they are mostly conveniently reviewed here under the heading of correlational studies. Both accounts make fascinating reading but few differences emerged between television viewers and non viewers across the wide variety of measures taken. The measures of aggression were fairly perfunctory especially in the case of Himmelweit who asked teachers to complete check lists on children, only one item of which related to aggression. However, no effect due to television was found. Schramm et al's results were a little different. In their first study young children (11-12 years old) in what was called "radio town" were more aggressive than in the "teletown", while no difference existed between older children. In their second study a weak trend was observed for heavy viewers of television to be more aggressive than light viewers.

For many people - including researchers - it is difficult to reconcile the marginal effects of television reported with the sheer ubiquity and richness of the medium. The belief that television must have antisocial effects has persisted. A flurry of studies followed. Only the most notable of these will be reviewed here.

Eron (1963) in a study of 875 children aged 8-9, found that boys who preferred violent TV programmes (as reported by their mothers) were more aggressive at school (as reported by their peers). There are numerous points that should be made about the research design but these will be taken up later. For the moment it should be immediately added that Eron also found a negative correlation between the amount of time spent watching television and aggressiveness. In this, Eron's results contradict those of Schramm. Reviewers have a simple choice: either Eron is right or Schramm is. We cannot conclude simply that both studies show a link between television and aggression. That would be dishonestly simplifying the findings. Other correlational data show a very curious pattern of inconsistencies. By and large where a link between television and aggression appears to exist, it is given by measures of violent programme preference rather than simply by exposure to violent programmes. It is worth noting that this in itself contradicts all of the experimental research where simply exposing subjects to violent films is claimed to increase aggressive responses -whether they like what they see or not is only rarely recorded.

Quite apart from this, the problem that other variables than those investigated, may explain apparent links between the mass media and aggression, plagues the correlational studies. McLeod, Atkin and Chaffee (1972) also produced evidence which ostensibly demonstrated a strong correlation between the amount of violence viewing and aggressiveness. This study based on a detailed survey over 600 adolescents in Maryland and Wisconsin found exposure to violent television positively correlated with self-reported aggression. The strongest association was in young girls. A number of other interesting findings were reported, for example that total television viewing, violence viewing and self reported aggression all declined from junior to senior high school and that boys watch considerably more violent television than girls. Unfortunately, the relationship found between television and aggression seems due to a failure to make allowance for sex and age. When the various groups formed by subdividing the sample on the basis of sex and school placement are considered, only one correlation out of eight approaches statistical significance (which is the kind of result that might be expected on a chance basis anyway). One other way of viewing their data is to consider the total number of correlations reported. Of the twenty described, nearly half were significant but only one was statistically significant in both the Maryland and the Wisconsin samples. Thus a fairly standard measure of reliability indicates that the findings are not very reliable.

McIntyre and Teevan (1972) carried out an even larger study on 2,270 adolescents in Maryland, measuring television viewing habits and various delinquent activities. Preferences for violent programmes were related to serious and aggressive delinquent acts rather than to petty delinquency. However, additionally, McIntyre and Teevan found that boys were more delinquent than girls while black and lower socio-economic groups contributed most to the overall deviancy. As with McCleod, Atkin and Chaffee, when age, sex and race were controlled, the reported correlations between television exposure and delinquency became considerably weaker and statistically insignificant, with only one exception, but again this is what would be expected on a chance basis.

Among the studies which show how other variables can produce spurious links between television and delinquency, perhaps that of Halloran, Brown and Chaney (1970) is one of the more telling. This study of 'delinquents' (children on probation) used two control groups: a middle class and a working class control group. In table after table clear differences emerge between delinquents and middle class controls and between working class and middle class controls. However, the crucial differences between delinquents and working class controls are only occasionally revealed and often seem gratuitous. Thus social class appears to explain more variance than delinquency does: an interesting point since so few studies take account of this. The researchers concluded "specific characteristics of delinquents' viewing behaviour can be accounted for in ways that have little bearing on the validation or disproof of simple, causal models". (Halloran, Brown and Chaney, 1970, p180)

Although opportunities to evaluate the introduction of television have become increasingly rare, a few studies have appeared over recent years. The most recent (Joy, Kimball and Zabrack, 1986) reports the results of a natural experiment taking place over a decade earlier when a small community hidden in a valley became able to receive television for the first time. The results suggested an increase in both physical and verbal aggression compared with two control communities. Interestingly, overall the results are interpreted more in terms of the general presence of television than its specific content (Williams, 1986), a conclusion reminiscent of Winn (1977) to which reply is difficult. A number of studies have attempted an aggregate approach to data on television's introduction to American cities during the 1950's. For example, Hennigan, Delrosario, Heath, Cook, Wharton and Colder (1982) concluded that television did not encourage violent crime but seemed to be associated with an increase in larceny - an effect, if it is reliable - which may point once more to other aspects of programming such as materialism rather than violence per se as the problematical issue.

Among studies which have focused on violence, arguably the most ambitious of correlational studies was executed by Belson (1978). This study of 1565 boys aged

13-16 in London set very high standards. It attempted to measure children's exposure to television violence in their earlier years and to link this to self-reported violent behaviour through a sophisticated system of matching heavy and light viewers of television violence. This matching was done according to over 200 different measures and thus attempts - reasonably well in fact - to overcome the serious problem that any correlation between delinquency and exposure to television violence could be due to a third variable like social class causing both. It would be churlish to criticise Belson for not being thorough enough in this search for third variables although his matching list is not exhaustive. Belson concludes that boys with high levels of exposure to television violence commit 49% more acts of serious violence than those who see little. He then goes on to list policy recommendations and suggests that violence should be reduced on television especially in "plays or films in which violence occurs in the context of close personal relations", "programmes presenting fictional violence of a realistic kind" and so on (eg p520). This sounds like the kind of impressive data supporting the specific recommendations needed to pinpoint controls on television. Unfortunately, closer examination of the vast amount of data Belson presents urges more caution. For example, the graphs for the full sample (pages 380-2) show that the results are far from as simple as his conclusions imply. In these graphs where exposure to television violence is plotted against violent behaviour, it is clear that the relationship is curvilinear. Thus very low viewers of television violence are slightly more aggressive than moderate viewers. More importantly very high viewers of television violence are less aggressive than the moderate to high exposure group (50% lower in fact!). Moreover in Belson's data, exposure to non violent television is also linked to aggressive behaviour, as indeed are comics/comic books and even newspaper readership.

One serious problem with Belson's results relates to the measures taken of television violence exposure. First of all, the list of programmes presented to children included some which had ceased to be broadcast when the children were 3 years old (Murdoch and McCron, 1979). Under these circumstances the validity of their responses may be doubted. Belson attempts to reassure critics on this point by demonstrating that responses were "reliable" (that on a second occasion boys produced the same responses). Although this is a conventional measure of reliability in research methods, it does not ensure validity. For example children might repeatedly assert that they are Martians, which would on this criterion then have to be considered a "reliable" response, but we might assume that the responses lacked validity. There are various ways round this problem of validity. One solution adopted by Milavsky (Milavsky, Kessler, Stipp and Rubens, 1982) - in a very comparable study to Belson's - is to present children with some fictitious television programme titles. If children claim to have seen these, then they may be considered invalid respondents. What is interesting about Milavsky's research is that he initially found a connection between television violence exposure and aggressivity but when he removed subjects who gave invalid responses, the correlation was reduced dramatically. In other words the link found by Belson and others may well be due to the inadequacy of the measures of television violence exposure taken. As a final point we should note that despite Belson's potential data base of 1565 subjects, the actual numbers contributing to the claimed link between television violence and serious acts of aggression must be considerably smaller. The cut off point for his matching samples was only 30 cases.

Some of the pitfalls in measuring media exposure are illustrated by a large survey carried out by Barlow and Hill (1985). This British study attempted to find out if children were exposing themselves to uncensored horror video films ('video-nasties'). This was a reasonable concern since they found that 40% of the 4,500 children surveyed claimed to have a video recorder at home. Barlow and Hill had been particularly worried that the lack of any regulatory system for this new medium allowed films to be available which had even been refused certification for cinema distribution by the British Board of Film Censors. They presented children with inter alia a five-page list of 113 film titles and asked them, if they had seen any of them on video, to rate them as 'great', 'just alright' or 'awful'. Their conclusions produced banner headlines in the press "Four children in ten watch video nasties", (*The Daily Express* 24 November, 1983), "The Rape of Young Minds" (*The Daily Mail* 24 November, 1983). Cumberbatch and Bates were suspicious that children might have quickly forgotten the instructions and simply rated films they had heard of or liked the sound of. To investigate this they reproduced Barlow and Hill's questionnaire but made some slight changes to some of the film titles. They made up fictitious video-nasty type film titles (*Zombies from beyond space, Cannibal Fang and Claw* and so on). The results from five classes of 11 year old children revealed that 68% of children claimed to have seen films which do not exist in any film guide. Morever, of the 72% of children who claimed to have seen an adult film, some 82% also claimed to have seen a fictitious film (Cumberbatch, 1984). Evidently Barlow and Hill's questionnaire was far from adequate quite apart from other bizarre features of their study (Barker, 1984; Tracey, 1984).

Although we must have reservations about Belson's work it remains far superior to anything else in this field. Curiously that of Eron et al. (Eron, Huesmann, Lefkowitz and Walter, 1972) is inferior in every respect and yet has been widely cited as definitive research linking television violence with aggression. Eron et al's contribution was a longitudinal study in which children's aggression and television violence exposure at 8-9 years old, and again 10 years later, were measured. Essentially they claimed a delayed action effect where early preference for television violence correlated with aggression at 18-19. While this is true for one of their measures of boys' aggression, two other measures did not show the relationship, while none of the measures showed this for girls. Later research by the group - Heusmann (1982) - failed to find this effect for either sex. Indeed at adulthood the correlation between television and aggression was slightly negative but no importance was attached to this. Unfortunately the measures used by Eron et al are far from adequate. Information on early television violence viewing in Eron's 1972 study was provided by parents who as Kay (1972) quickly pointed out are not likely to provide very valid data. Parents might for example guess that aggressive programmes might be preferred by an aggressive child. Indeed the possibility that aggressive personality explains early television violence viewing and later aggression is not taken seriously - but neither was it tested by Belson, until he was criticised for this oversight (see Gunter 1983; Belson, 1985). The measures of aggression used are also troublesome on two counts. First of all they do not measure aggression alone, but also assertive behaviour as perceived by class mates (for example "who often says 'give me that!'". "who does things that bothers others?", "who does not obey the teacher?"). The second problem is the use of peer ratings when children had left school - an unknown number would be rating their class mates from when they were last at school together. Only half of the original sample provided data in the follow up study. The results may only show that aggressive children are not easily forgotten. In any case we should not be surprised if aggressive children grow up to be aggressive. (eg Olweus, 1980; Spivack, Marcus and Swift, 1986)

Later longitudinal studies (eg Eron 1982; Eron, Huesmann, Brice, Fisher and Mermelstein 1983, Huesmann and Eron, 1986) are no less crude in the measures taken although analyses became increasingly sophisticated. Television violence was inferred only from a list of a child's eight favourite shows. A television violence score was calculated by multiplying these programmes by their "violence content" (a 1-5 scale) and by how often the child claimed to watch them (on a 1-3 scale). "Violence content" is unfortunately not defined but appeared to include all violence including cartoons. Measures of aggression were similar to the earlier research but involved different methodologies at different ages, which clearly produced differences in rated aggression. Although the data are exceptionally weak, the most troublesome aspect of the research lies in the failure to consider any other explanation for the results than that television violence causes aggression. Thus the well known evidence from Milavsky on invalid respondents contributing generously to the link is ignored, as is Gunter's (1983) concern that aggressive personality causes preferences for violent television. In the various reports a number of other variables produce significant correlates both with aggression and with television behaviour pointing to possible explanations of the link between the two, but, unlike Belson, the researchers made little attempt to remove these as third variables. One exception is reading achievement, which as Eron (1982) noted reduces the correlation between television viewing and aggression from +0.245 to +0.134. It must be suspected that other variables would have similar effects and, taken together, might well account for much of the remaining relationship.

Examining the pattern of research findings reported by Huesmann and Eron (1986) a number of curious contradictions exist. Huesmann (1984) had reported on the results of a three year panel study in the USA and Finland. Early TV violence viewing predicted later aggression in girls in the USA but not in boys and in neither sex in Israel. Later analysis attempted a more sophisticated approach taking into account identification with television characters plus the amount of violence watched. This produced a significant contribution to aggression for boys in both Finland and Israel but not for girls. However, aggressive children of both sexes were more likely to identify with television characters than were low aggressive children. Of course post hoc explanations are always possible for mixed success in producing consistent results and indeed many reviews consider the various data to show a consistent pattern (eg Turner, Hesse and Peterson-Lewis, 1986: Liebert and Sprafkin, 1988). However, some caution needs to be exercised in interpreting such uneven data. The various results may be taken as supporting the hypothesis that television violence causes aggression but the evidence is "weak and inconsistent" (Freedman, 1988, p158).

Although the studies of Eron and his associates have probably contributed little to our understanding of the influence of television, their concerns about its harmful effects have stimulated some interesting experiments to protect children from it. For example Huesmann, Eron, Kleen, Price and Fisher (1983) asked school children to write essays on why television violence is bad and unreal. This not only reduced aggression as rated by peers but reduced the correlation between television violence viewing and aggression. Similar experiments are reported in Singer, Zuckerman and Singer (1980), Anderson (1983) Sprafkin, Swift and Hess (1983), Sprafkin, Gadow and Kant (1988) and Eron (1986). While these may not tell us anything about the usual effects of television and may not even have anything to do with the effects of television per se, it would seem a most promising line to follow. After all children should be taught to understand both television and their own socialisation, whatever the relationship between the two may be.

Discussions and Conclusions

This review has focused on some of the methodological problems with research in this field. Doubtlessly better studies could be done and indeed should be done. Nevertheless the overriding inadequacies of the research are primarily conceptual.

First of all researchers and reviewers alike have difficulty in handling non significant results. These are rarely part of any scientific debate and indeed are unlikely to be published at all (Greenwald, 1975; Melton, 1962; Smith, 1980; Westland, 1978). However, in the correlational studies the vast data show a preponderance of non-significant findings which should alert us to the danger of falsely concluding that there are genuine specific effects of mass media violence upon society. Few empirical studies are worth a second mention, but Belson for example finds no evidence that high exposure to television violence reduces boys' respect for authority, or that it desensitises them, makes them less considerate of others, produces sleep disturbance or (in an earlier study, Belson, 1975) is associated with stealing. Belson's findings contradict many previous studies. Thus the convention of reviewers to consider only significant results is rather misleading.

The second conceptual problem in the research is that it focuses on the possible effects of the media as a unidimensional process. It is true that over the years more attention has been paid to possible prosocial effects (eg Leibert, Sprafkin and Davidson, 1982; Liss, Reinhardt and Fredriksen, 1983; Rushton, 1979; Sprafkin, Gadow and Kant, 1988). However the problem of unidimensional thinking is well illustrated in the conclusions to a recent review by Berkowitz (1984). He concludes:

> The chance that only one individual in 100,000 will exhibit overt aggression as a result of the depicted violence means 100 more violent acts will occur in an audience of 10,000,000. Whatever the exact numbers, our society has to decide whether the benefits of portrayed aggression outweigh the cost. (Berkowitz 1984, p424)

Even if it were accepted that research supported this probability of one individual in 100,000 being more likely to exhibit overt aggression, the aggressor is only part of the equation of violence as a social problem. It cannot be translated into more violent acts in this simple way. Are victims more or less vulnerable because of violence on television? Are witnesses more or less likely to report antisocial behaviour or even intervene because of violence on television? And what are the effects on the police, the judiciary or the legislature? Do governments become more or less active against crime and violence because of violence on television or the public concern over it? Since we have precious little evidence on these processes which 'cause' crime and alter the criminal statistics, society may well find it difficult to decide in the way that Berkowitz thinks it should. Moreover, the use of the term 'violence' as if it were an easily defined homogeneous group of actions is a nonsense. 'Violence' on television can cover an enormous diversity of acts taking place in different contexts for different reasons and with quite different messages for different viewers.

Violence has long played a vital role in the arts and is used with various dramatic effects by those who create our cultural forms (Fraser 1974). How successful a film producer is in conveying that violence is something to be condoned or condemned, to be appalled by or laughed at, is obviously an empirical question only answered ultimately by interrogating the audience. However the assumption made by so much research is that these distinctions do not exist for the viewer. For example, George Gerbner (1972) and Halloran and Croll (1972) in describing the violence profile of television in the USA and the UK respectively do not even take into account programme genre, so that *Tom and Jerry* appears as one of the most violent programmes on television - a view not shared by the public (Howitt and Cumberbatch, 1974). Current research at least is attempting to address this issue in a more subtle way by examining how violence is presented in different types of film and television programmes (Cumberbatch, Hardy, Lee and Jones, 1987) and how viewers respond differently according to the different contexts in which violence is presented (Gunter 1985). At the theoretical level the notion that violence has a simple unidimensional effect is being increasingly challenged as trite by the growing tradition of "uses and gratifications" research, which seeks to identify the dynamic relationship that particular individuals with particular needs and world views may enjoy with the mass media (eg Frank and Greenberg, 1980; Palmgreen, 1984; Rosengren, Wenner and Palmgreen, 1985; Rubin, 1984; Taylor and Mullan, 1986; Zillman and Bryant, 1985).

A third conceptual weakness lies in the psychological processes hypothesised to operate in any mediation of television violence. Until recently these have been remarkably crude with inevitable consequence in terms of the research designs adopted. Fortunately current developments in cognitive social psychology especially those pursuing the idea of complex scripts for social behaviour are at last penetrating the debates about television violence (eg. Berkowitz 1986; Huesmann 1986; Josephson 1988; Singer and Singer 1981). For example, imitation as developed by Bandura (eg 1983) as a theory of media effect falls short of a psychological explanation of the processes involved. The reason is that imitation is not a process but an effect - as measured by matching responses of the observer to the model. It does not explain the dynamics of how these behaviours arise. Even the concept of identification with a television character has not been explored in terms of its possibilities as a process contributing to the large constellation of attitudes, assumptions, expectations, beliefs, etc., that might be influenced (Barker, 1989). The only research to date which has attempted to tease out how identification with a film character might influence the various dimensions of moral judgement made by children has concluded surprisingly that no effect could be demonstrated (Howitt and Cumberbatch 1975, Cumberbatch and Howitt 1974). Clearly a lot more needs to be done to develop theory in this area.

It is unlikely that research will do much to reduce controversy about crime and violence in the mass media, but future studies could usefully address the question of why it is such a controversial topic. Failure to consider this has provided the fourth major conceptual weakness in research to date. However two recent books are worthy of note in illuminating the politics of research and campaigning in this field: Rowland (1983) on the policy uses of communications research on television violence and Barker (1984a) on the campaign to ban horror comic books. Political issues are raised elsewhere. For example, Liebert, Sprafkin, Davidson (1982) devote a good proportion of their review to the politics of the massive 1972 U.S. Surgeon General's Enquiry into Television and Social Behaviour. Additionally Barker (1984b) gathers together an interesting collection of essays on the campaign to control "video nasties" in Britain. No doubt much has to do with the boundaries of public taste but this remains fairly unexplored as a research issue. (Morris 1987)

What is still lacking is any close analysis of the evident public concerns about mass media violence which is the fifth major conceptual weakness worth noting. Early studies noted various inconsistencies in public opinion. For example, while polls show that the majority view is that there is too much violence on television, the number of spontaneous complaints to the broadcasting authorities specifically mentioning violence is minuscule - figures of less than 1% have been reported (eg Howitt and Cumberbatch, 1975). The Broadcasting Research Departments of the BBC and the IBA carry out regular surveys of public opinion show only a fraction of television programmes are disapproved of by a tiny minority of viewers (Gunter and Wober 1988) or indeed spontaneously in group discussions by the general public (Cumberbatch 1988). Nevertheless when the Director General of the BBC in December 1985 invited the public to write in with any complaints about objectionable scenes on television, some 4,000 people responded - 90% of whom complained about television violence. Even so despite the request to identify particular programmes or series that they objected to only 3% quoted specific incidents. (McGregor, 1986)

What is also curious is that when people mentioned specific programmes the most cited were "the news" (18%) followed by "films" (17%) followed by American programmes generally. This raises the question of whether concerns about television violence more accurately reflect concerns about violence . This was the conclusion reached in a recent study of television news coverage of the year long miners' strike (March 1984 - March 1985). Here public opinion polls showed that over 70% of people described the strike as "very violent" while a further 26% thought it "fairly violent". And yet when asked what issues had received too much coverage in the news, 59% of people spontaneously mentioned the violence (Cumberbatch, McGregor, Brown and Morrison, 1986). This presents something of a dilemma for broadcasters - would they be criticised for not showing violence? The news is of course rather different from fiction where the violence can - to a large extent - be tailored to audience tastes. However, while crime and violence in the news may not be any more or less harmful than in fiction, any discussion of the news must bring in other considerations than simply the viewer's consequent aggressivity. It is unfortunate that such discussions that take place within broadcasting about what to show and how, are rarely part of public knowledge (eg Redfern 1988). The perspective as given by the broadcaster's guidelines (*The Portrayal of Violence on Television* BBC/IBA, 1980, *Producers Guidelines* BBC, 1989) reflect a professional concern which needs to be part of any debate. As the guidelines advise, "In deciding whether a moment of violence should be portrayed in any programme, and in what manner it should be presented, the basic aim must always be ...... to sharpen and not to blunt the sensitivities of the viewer." It is difficult to disagree with this aim but the consequences for the viewer may not always be those intended and certainly are not easy to predict. Despite the lack of precision in the guidelines, they offer an obvious starting point for applied psychological research and yet only Howitt and Cumberbatch seem to have reported empirical investigation of them. (Howitt and Cumberbatch, 1972; Cumberbatch and Howitt, 1974, Cumberbatch and Howitt, 1975)

Whatever the role of the mass media in our lives it has become an important focus for research and has exposed a variety of methodological weaknesses in our research tools. Most importantly the research endeavours indicate that conceptual limitations provide a major barrier to understanding the media and a major rift between researchers and practitioners. Debates about the effects of television violence inevitably draw in other concerns - about rising crime, broadcasting freedom, the vulnerability of children, parental rights, media obligations and professional standards on television and sundry other issues. It is perhaps not surprising that the question of whether television violence influences violence in real life remains inherently controversial. At the end of the day the research evidence needs to be assessed in terms of what potential policy recommendations are inherent in the various data. Arguably these are insufficiently robust to allow a firm conclusion about television violence as studied. However, an additional concern is that research has failed to establish specific types of programme as more problematical than others. Singer and Singer's recent conclusion is exceptional: "Later aggressive behavior was predicted by earlier heavy viewing of public television's fast paced *Sesame Street* as well as more violent cartoons, *Superheroes* and *Woody Woodpecker*". (Singer and Singer, 1986 p113)

This is most troubling. *Sesame Street* was developed with psychologists as an attempt to produce quality programming that educates and entertains. Liebert and Sprafkin (1988) enthuse about the project under the heading: "*Sesame Street*: Anatomy of a Success" (Liebert and Sprafkin, 1988, p214). Many American researchers who contribute most the research evidence on the effects of television violence are also very concerned about improving the quality of chidren's broadcasting. It remains to be seen how they will respond to Singer's perhaps naive honesty. No doubt they will concur "if only he hadn't mentioned *Sesame Street!*" But what if "fast paced" programmes rather than violence are the problem? We simply do not know. Research evidence leaves practitioners pretty much stranded, but if they are thoughtfully so, then it's not a bad thing.

KEY REFERENCES

ADAIR, J. G. (1973) *The Human Subject: the social psychology of the psychological experiment* Boston, Mass, Little, Brown.

ANDERSON, J. A. (1983) 'Television literacy and the critical viewer' in: J. Bryant & D. R. Anderson (eds). *Children's Understanding of Television* New York, Academic Press pp.297-330.

ANDISON, F. R. (1977) 'TV violence and viewer aggression: a cumulation of study results 1956-1979' *Public Opinion Quarterly* 41(3), pp.314-331.

BANDURA, A. (1973) *Aggression: A Social Learning Analysis* Englewood Cliffs, New Jersey, : Prentice-Hall.

- (1983) 'Psychological mechanisms of aggression'. in: R. G. Green and C. I. Donnerstein (eds) *Aggression, Theoretical and Empirical Reviews: vol 1 Theoretical and Methodological Issues* New York, Academic Press pp.1-40.

BANDURA, A. & HUSTON ALETHA, C. (1961) 'Identification as a process of incidental learning' *Journal of Abnormal and Social Psychology* 63 pp.311-318.

BANDURA, A., ROSS, D. & ROSS, S. A. (1961) 'Transmission of aggression through Imitation of aggressive models} *Journal of Abnormal and Social Psychology* 63, pp.575-582.

- (1963a) 'Imitation of film-mediated aggresive models' *Journal of Abnormal and Social Psychology* 66, pp.3-11.

- (1963b) 'Vicarious reinforcement and imitative learning'. *Journal of Abnormal and Social Psychology* 67, pp601-607.

BARKER, M. (1984a) *A Haunt of Fears*. London, Pluto.

- (ed) (1984b) *The Video Nasties* London, Pluto.

- (1989) *Comics, Influences, Ideology* Manchester, Manchester University Press (in press).

BARLOW, G. & HILL, A. (1985) *Video Violence and Children* London, Hodder & Stoughton.

BARON JONES, N. & REISS, P S. (1985) 'Same time, next year: Aggregate analyses of the mass media and video behavior' *American Sociological Review* 50, pp.347-363.

BELSON, W. A. (1975) *Juvenile Theft: the causal factors* London, Harper & Row.

- (1978) *Television Violence and the Adolescent Boy* Farnborough, Teakfield.

- (1985) 'The effects of television violence' *Bulletin of the British Psychological Society* 38, pp.120-122.

BERKOWITZ, L. (1962) *Aggression: A Social Psychological Analysis* New York, McGraw-Hill.

- (1968) 'Impulse, aggression and the gun' *Psychology Today* 2(4), pp.18-22.

- (1971) 'The "weapons effect", Demand characteristics and the myth of the compliant subject' *Journal of Personality and Social Psychology* 20(3), pp.332-338.

- (1984) 'Some effects of thoughts on anti- and prosocial influences of media events: A cognitive-neoassociation analysis' *Psychological Bulletin* 95(3), pp.410-427.

- (1986) 'Situational influences on reactions to observed violence' *Journal of Social Issues* 42(3), pp.93-103.

BERKOWITZ, L & GEEN, R. G. (1966) 'Female violence and the cue properties of available targets' *Journal of Personality and Social Psychology* 3, pp.525-30.

- (1967) 'Stimulus qualities of the target of aggression' *Journal of Personality and Social Psychology* 5, pp.364-368.

BERKOWITZ, L. & LE PAGE, A. (1967) 'Weapons as aggression-eliciting stimuli' *Journal of Personality and Social Psychology* 7, pp.202-207.

BERKOWITZ, L. & RAWLINGS, E. (1963) 'Effects of film violence on inhibitions against subsequent aggression' *Journal of Abnormal and Social Psychology* 66, pp.405-12.

BERMAN, A. L. (1988) 'Fictional depiction of suicide in television films amd imitation effects' *The American Journal of Psychiatry* 145(10), pp.982-986.

BLURTON JONES, N. (1976) 'Rough and tumble play among nursery school children' in: J. S. Bruner, A. Jolly and K. Sylva (eds). *Play: Its Role in Development and Evolution* Harmondsworth, Penguin. pp.352-363.

BORDEN, R J. (1975) 'Witnessed aggression' *Journal of Personality and Social Psychology* 31, pp.567-573.

BRITISH BROADCASTING CORPORATION (1989) *Producers Guidelines* London, BBC.

BROWN, R. L. (1970) 'Approaches to the historical development of mass media studies' in: J Tunstall *Media Sociology* London, Constable. pp.41-57.

BRYANT, J., CARVETH, R. A. & BROWN, D. (1981) 'Television viewing and anxiety' *Journal of Communication* 31, pp.106-119.

BUSS, A. H., BOOKER, A., & BUSS, E. (1972) 'Firing a weapon and aggression' *Journal of Personality and Social Psychology* 22, pp.96-302.

COUGHLIN, E. K. (1985) 'Is violence on TV harmful to our health? Some scholars, a vocal minority say no' *Chronicle of Higher Education* March, pp.65-71.

CRESSEY, P. G. & THRASHER, F. M. (1933) *Boys, Movies and City Streets* New York, Macmillan

CUMBERBATCH, G. (1984) 'Sorting out little white lies from nasty pieces of research' *The Guardian* 25 April 1984.
- (1988) 'TV violence : Too violent?' *Broadcast* 19 February 1988, p 25.

CUMBERBATCH, G. & BEARDSWORTH, A. (1976) 'Criminals victims and mass communications' in: E. G. Viano (Ed) *Victims and Society* Washington DC, Visage. Pp.72-90.

CUMBERBATCH, G., HARDY, G., LEA, M. & JONES, I (1987) *The Portrayal of Violence on British Television* London, BBC.

CUMBERBATCH, G. & HOWITT, D. (1974) 'Identification with aggressive television characters and children's moral judgements' in: J. Dewitt & W. W. Hartup (eds) *Determinants and Origins of Aggressive Behaviour* The Hague, Mouton pp.517-523.

CUMBERBATCH, G., McGREGOR, R., BROWN, B. & MORRISON, D. (1986) *Television and the miners' strike* London, Broadcasting Research Unit.

CUMBERBATCH, G. & MORGAN, B. (1985) 'The police officer' in: W. T. Singleton (ed) *The Study of Real Skills* Vol 4 Lancaster, MTP Press.

CUMBERBATCH, G., JONES, I. & LEE, M. (1988). 'Measuring violence on television' *Current Psychological Research and Reviews* 7, 1, pp.8-23.

DOLLARD, J., DOOB, L. W., MILLER, N. E., MOWRER, O. H. & SEARS, R. R. (1939) *Frustration and Aggression* New Haven, Conn, Yale University Press.

DONERSTEIN, E. & BERKOWITZ, L. (1981) 'Victim reactions in aggressive erotic films as a factor in violence against women' *Journal of Personality and Social Psychology* 41, pp.710-724.

ERON, L. D. (1963) 'Relationship of TV viewing habits and aggressive behavior in children' *Journal of Abnormal and Social Psychology* 67, pp.193-196.

ERON, L. D., LEFTKOWITZ, M. M., HUESMANN, L. R. & WALDER, L. O. (1972) 'Does television violence cause aggression?' *American Psychologist* 27, pp.253-263.

ERON, L. D. (1982) 'Parent-child Interaction, television violence and aggression in children' *American Psychologist* 37(2), pp.197-211.

ERON, L. D., HUESMANN, L. R., BRICE, P., FISHER, P. & MERMELSTEIN, R. (1983) 'Age trends in the development of aggression, sex-typing and related television habits' *Developmental Psychology* (19), pp.71-77.

EYSENCK, H. J. & NIAS, D. K. (1978) *Sex, Violence and the Media* London, Maurice Temple Smith.

FESHBACH, S. (1955) 'The drive-reducing function of fantasy behavior' *Journal of Abnormal and Social Psychology* 50, pp.3-11.

FESHBACH, S. (1963) 'The stimulating versus cathartic effects of a vicarious aggressive activity' *Journal of Abnormal and Social Psychology* 63 pp.381-5.

FESHBACH, S. & SINGER, R. D. (1971) 'Television and Aggression: An Experimental Field Study' San Francisco, Jossey-Bass.

FRANK, R. E. & GREENBERG, M. G. (1980) *The Public's use of Television: Who Watches and Why* London, Sage.

FRASER, C. (1974) *Violence in the Arts* London, Cambridge University Press.

FRIEDMAN, N. (1967) *The Social Nature of Psychological Research: The Psychological Experiment as a Social Interaction* New York, Basic Books.

FRIEDMAN, J. L. (1984) 'Effects of television violence on aggression' *Psychological Bulletin* 96(2), pp.227-246.
- (1986) 'Television violence and aggression: a rejoinder' *Psychological Bulletin* 100(3), pp.372-378.
- (1988) 'Television violence and aggression: what the evidence shows' in: S. Oskamp (ed) *Television as a social issue. Applied Social Psychology Annual No 8* Newbury Park, California, Sage. pp.144-162.

FRIEDRICH-COFER, L. & HUSTON, A. C. (1986) 'Television violence and aggression: The debate continues' *Psychological Bulletin* 100 (3), pp.364-371.

FRODI, A. (1975) 'The effect of exposure to weapons on aggressive behavior from a cross-cultural perspective' *International Journal of Psychology* 10, pp.283-292.

GADOW, K. D. & SPRAFKIN, J. (1989) 'Field experiments of television violence' *Pediatrics* 83 March (In press).

GEEN, R. G & O'NEALL, E. (1969) 'Activation of cue-ellicited aggression by general arousal' *Journal of Personality and Social Psychology* 11(3), pp.289-292.

GERBNER, G. (1972) 'Violence in television drama: trends and symbolic functions' in: G. A. Comstock and E. A. Rubenstein (eds) *Television and Social Behavior, Vol 1, Media Content and Control* Washington DC, US Government Printing Office. pp.28-187.

GERBNER, G., GROSS, L., ELEEY, M. E., JACKSDON BEECK, M., JEFFRIES-FOX, S. & SIGNORIELLI, N. (1977) 'Television violence profile No 8.' *Journal of Communication* 27, pp.171-180.

GOULD, M. S. & SHATTER, D. (1986) 'The impact of suicide in television movies: evidence of imitations' *The New England Journal of Medicine* 315, pp.690-693

GREENWALD, A. G. (1975) 'Consequences of prejudice against the null hypothesis' *Psychological Bulletin* 82, pp.1-20.

GUNTER, B. (1985) *Dimensions of Television Violence* Aldershot, Gower Press.

- (1987) *Television and the fear of crime* London, John Libbey.

GUNTER, B. & WOBER, M. (1983) 'Television viewing and public trust' *British Journal of Social Psychology*, 22, pp.174-176.

- (1988) *Violence on Television: what the viewers think* London, John Libbey.

HALLORAN, J. D., BROWN, R. L. & CHANEY, D. C. (1970) *Television and Delinquency* Leicester, Leicester University Press.

HALLORAN, J. D. & CROLL, P. (1972) 'Television programmes in Great Britain' in G. A. Comstock and E. A. Rubenstein (eds) *Television and Social Behaviour Vol 1: Content and Control* Washington DC, US Government Print Office. pp.415-492.

HARTLEY, R. (1964) *A Review and Evaluation of Recent Studies on the Impact of Violence* New York, CBS Inc. pp.19-20.

HAWKINS, R. & PINGREE, S. (1980) 'Some processes in the cultivation effect' *Communication Research* 7, pp.193-226.

HEAROLD, S. (1986) 'A synthesis of 1043 effects of television on social behavior' in: G. Comstock (ed) *Public Communications and Behaviour : Volume 1* pp.65-133. New York, Academic Press

HEATH, A., JOWELL, R. & CURTICE, J. (1985) *How Britain Votes* Oxford, Pergamon.

HENNIGAN, K. M., DELROSARIO, M. L., HEATH, L., COOK, T. D., WHARTON, J. D. & CALDER, B J. (1982) 'Impact of the introduction of television crime in the United States. Empirical findings and theoretical implications' *Journal of Personality and Social Psychology* 42, pp.461-477.

HICKS, D. (1968) 'Imitation and retention of film-mediated aggressive peer and adult models' *Journal of Personality and Social Psychology* 2, pp.97-100.

HIMMELWEIT, H. T. OPENHEIM, A. N. & VINCE, P. (1958) *Television and the Child: An Empirical Study of the Effect of Television on the Young* London, Oxford University Press.

HIRSCH, P. (1980) 'The scary world of the non viewer and other anomalies: Re-analysis of Gerbener et al's findings on the cultivation hypothesis' *Communication Research* 7, pp.403-456.

- (1981a) 'On not learning from one's own mistakes: A re-analysis of Gerbner et al's findings on cultivation analysis. Part II' *Communications Research* 8, pp.3-37.

- (1981b) Distinguishing good speculation from bad theory. *Communications Research*, 8, 73-96.

HOUGH, M. & MAYHEW, P. (1985) 'Taking account of crime: Key findings from the 1984 British Crime Survey' *Research Studies* No 85, London, HMSO.

HOWITT, D. (1972) 'Effects of aggressive modelling upon non-initiative aggression' *Catalogue of Selected Documents in Psychology* 2, pp.114-15.

- (1982) *Mass Media and Social Problems* Oxford, Pergamon.

HOWITT, D. & CUMBERBATCH, G. (1971) *Experiment transparency in a study of the Effects of Filmed Agression* Unpublished manuscript: Centre for Mass Communication Research, University of Leicester, England.

- (1972) 'Affective feeling for a film character and evaluation of an anti-social act' *British Journal of Social and Clinical Psychology* 11, pp.102-108.

- (1974) 'Audience perceptions of violent television content. *Communication Research* 1, pp.204-223.

- (1975) *Mass Media Violence and Society* London, Elek.

HUESMAN, L. R. (1982) 'Television violence and aggressive behaviour' in: D. Pearl, L. Bouthilet and J. Lazar (eds) *Television and Behaviour* Vol 2 Washington DC, NIMH.
- (1986) 'Psychological processes promoting the relation between exposure to media violence and aggressive behaviour by the viewer' *Journal of Social Issues* 42(3), pp.125-139.
HUESMANN, L. R., ERON, L., KLEEN, L., BRICE, P. & FIOHER, P. (1983) 'Mitigating the imitation of aggressive behaviours by changing children's attitudes to media violence' *Journal of Personality and Social Psychology* 44, pp.899-910
HUESMANN, L. R. & ERON, L. D. (eds) (1986) *Television and the Aggressive Child : A Cross-National Comparison* Hillsdale, New Jersey, Lawrence Elbaum Associates.
HUESMAN, L. R., KAGERSPETY, K. & ERON, L. D. (1984) 'Intervening variables in the TV violence-aggression relation' *Developmental Psychology* 20, pp.746-775.
HUESMAN, L. R. & MALAMUTH, N. M. (eds) (1986) 'Media Violence and Antisocial Behaviour' *Journal of Social Issues* 42(3).
HUGHES, M. (1980) 'The fruits of cultivation analysis' *Public Opinion Quarterly* 44, pp.287-302.
HUSTON - STEIN, A., FOX, S., GREEN, D., WATKINS, B. A. & WHITAKER, J. (1981) 'The effects of TV action and violence on childrens behavior' *The Journal of Genetic Psychology* 138, pp.183-191.
JOSEPHSON, W. L. (1987) 'Television violence and children's aggression: testing the priming, social script and disinhibition predictions' *Journal of Personality and Social Psychology* 53(5) pp.882-890.
JOY, L. A., KIMBALL, M. M. & ZABRACK, M. L. (1986) 'Television and aggressive behaviour' in T. M. Williams (ed) *The Impact of Television: a Natural Experiment Involving Three Towns* New York, Academic Press.
KAY, H. (1972) 'Weakness in the television-causes-aggression analysis by Eron et al' *American Psychologist* 27, pp.970-973.
KESSLER, R. C. & STIPP, H. (1984) 'The impact of fictional television suicide stories on US fatalities: a replication' *American Journal of Sociology* 90(1), pp.157-167.
KESSLER, R. C., DOWNEY, G., MILAVSKY, J. R. & STIPP, H. (1988) 'Clustering of teenage suicides after television stories about suicides: a re-consideration' *The American Journal of Psychiatry* 145(11), pp.1379-1383.
KILLIAS, M. (1983) 'Mass medias: peur du crime et politique criminelle' *Revue Internationale de Criminologe et de Police Technique* 36(4), pp.60-71.
KNIVETON, B. H. & STEPHENSON, G. M. (1970) 'The effect of pre-experience on imitation of an aggressive film model' *British Journal of Social and Clinical Psychology* 9, pp.31-36.
LARSEN, O. N. (ed) (1968) *Violence and the Mass Media* New York, Harper and Row.
LESYNA, K. & PHILLIPS, D. P. (1989) 'Suicide and The Media: Research and Policy Implications' in R. Diekstra *The World Health Organization for Preventive Strategies on Suicide: A WHO State of the Art Publication* (In Press).
LEVEY, L. (1967) 'Awareness, learning and the beneficient subject as expert witness' *Journal of Personality and Social Psychology* 6, pp.365-70.
LEYENS, J. P., CAMINO, L., PARKE, R. D. & BERKOWITZ, L. (1975) 'The effect of movie violence on aggression in a field setting as a function of group dominance and cohesion' *Journal of Personality and Social Psychology* 32, pp.346-360.
LEYENS, J. P. & PARKE, R. D. (1975) 'Aggressive slides can induce a weapon's effect' *European Journal of Social Psychology* 5, pp.229-236.
LIEBERT, R. M., NEALE, J. M. & DAVIDSON, E. S. (1973) *The Early Window: Effects of Television on Children and Youths* Elmsford, New York, Pergamon.
LIEBERT, R. M. & SPRAFKIN, J. N. (1988) *The Early Window: Effects of Television on Children and Youths* (3rd Edn) New York: Pergamon Press.
LINNE, O. (1976) 'The viewer's aggression as a function of a variously edited TV film' *Communications* 1, pp.101-111.
LISKA, A. E., SANCHIRO, A. & REED, M. D. (1988) 'Fear of crime and constrained behavior specifying and estimating a reciprocal effects model' *Social Forces* 66(3) pp.827-837.
LISS, M. A., REINHARDT, L. C. & FREDRIKSEN, S. (1983) 'TV heroes: the impact of rhetoric and deeds' *Journal of Applied Developmental Psychology* 4(2), pp.175-187.
McGREGOR, R. (1986) 'Television violence: corresponding claims' *The Listener* 26 June 1986, pp.26-27.
McGUIRE, W. J. (1986) 'The myth of massive media impact: savagings and salvagings' *Public Communication and Behavior* 1, pp.175-257.
McHAN, E. J. (1985) 'Imitation of aggression by Lebanese children' *Journal of Social Psychology* 125(5), pp.613-617.

56

McINTYRE, J. J. & TEEVAN, J. J. (1972) 'Television violence and deviant behavior' in: *TV and Social Behavior, Vol 3* Washington DC, US Government Printing Office.

McLEOD, J. M., ATKIN, C. K. & CHAFFEE, S. H. (1972) 'Adolescents, parents and television use: Self report and other report measures from Maryland and Wisconsin samples' in: G. G. Comstock & E. A. Rubenstein *TV and Social Behavior, Vol 3* Washington DC, US Government Printing Office.

McQUAIL, D. (1969) *Towards a Sociology of Mass Communications* London, Collier-Macmillan.

- (1987) *Mass Communication Theory : an introduction* London, Sage

MELTON, A. W. (1962) 'Editorial' *Journal of Experimental Psychology* 64. pp.553-557.

MENDELSOHN, H. (1983) 'Using the mass media for crime prevention' (cited by Wober & Gunter, 1988).

MESSNER, S. F. (1986) 'Television violence and violent crime: an aggregate analysis' *Social Problems* 33(3), pp.218-235.

MILAVSKY, J R, KESSLER, R. C., STIPP, H. H. & RUBENS, W. S. (1982) *Television and Aggression: A Panel Study* New York, Academic Press.

MILGRAM, S. (1965) 'Some conditions of obedience and disobedience to authority' *Human Relations* 18, pp.57-76.

- (1974) *Obedience to Authority* New York, Harper and Row.

MILGRAM, S. & SHOTLAND, R. L. (1973) *Television and Antisocial Behavior: Field Experiments* New York, Academic Press.

MORGAN, M. (1983) 'Symbolic victimization and real-world fear' *Human Communication Research* 9(2), pp.146-157.

MORRIS, C. (1987) *Drawing the Line* London, BBC Books.

MUELLER, C. W., DONNERSTEIN, E. & HALLAM, J. (1983) 'Violent films and prosocial behaviour' *Journal of Personality and Social Psychology* 9, pp.83-89.

MURDOCK, G. & McCRON, R, (1979) 'The Television and Delinquency Debate' *Screen Education* 30, Spring.

N.I.M.H.(1982) *Television and Behavior: Ten years of Scientific Progress and Implications for the Eighties* Rockville, MO, National Institute of Mental Health.

NOBLE, G. (1975) *Children in Front of the Small Screen* London, Constable.

OLWEUS, D. (1980) 'The consistency issue in personality psychology revisited - with special reference to aggression' *British Journal of Social and Clinical Psychology* 19, pp.377-390.

ORNE, M. T. (1969) 'Demand characteristics and the concept of quasi-experimental controls' in: R. Rosenthal and R. Rosnow (eds) *Artifact in Behavioral Research* New York, Academic Press. Pp.143-179.

ORNE, M. T. & HOLLAND, C. H. (1968) 'On the ecological validity of laboratory deceptions' *International Journal of Psychiatry* 6, pp.282-293.

PAGE, M. & SCHEIDT, R. (1971) 'The elusive weapons effect: Demand awareness, evaluation and slightly sophisticated subjects' *Journal of Personality and Social Psychology* 20, pp.304-318.

PARKE, R. D., BERKOWITZ, L., LEYENS, J. P., WEST, S. G. & SEBASTIAN, R. J . (1977) 'Some effects of violent and non-violent movies on the behavior of juvenile delinquents' in: L Berkowitz (ed) *Advances in Experimental Social Psychology* Vol 10. New York, Academic Press.

PATTERSON, G. R., LITTMAN, R. A. & BRICKER, W. (1967) 'Assertive behavior in children: A step towards a theory of aggression' *Monographs of Social Research in Child Development* 32.

PHILLIPS, D. P. (1982) 'The impact of fictitional television stories on US adult fatalities: new evidence on the effect of the mass media on violence' *American Journal of Sociology* 87(6), pp.1340-59.

- (1983) 'The impact of mass media violence on US homicides' *American Sociological Review* 48, pp.560-68.

PHILLIPS, D. P. & CASTERSEN, L. L. (1986) 'Clustering of teenage suicides after television stories about suicide' *The New England Journal of Medicine* 315, pp.685-689.

PHILLIPS, D.P. & HENSLEY, J. E. (1984) 'When violence is rewarded or punished: the impact of mass media stories on homicide' *Journal of Communication* 34, pp.101-116.

PHILLIPS, D. P. & PAIGHT, D. J. (1987) 'The impact of televised movies about suicide : a replicative study' *The New England Journal of Medicine* 317, pp.809-811.

PIEPE, A., CROUCH, J. & EMERSON, M. (1977) 'Violence and television' *New Society* 41, pp.536-538.

PILIAVIN, I. A., DOVIDION, J. F., GAERNTNER, S. L. & CLARK, R. D. (1981) *Emergency Intervention* New York, Academic Press.

PLATT, S. (1987) 'The Aftermath of Angie's Overdose: Is soap (opera) damaging your health?' *British Medical Journal* 294, pp.954-957.

REDFERN, S. (1988) Violence and the media. London, UK: BBC Publications.

ROSENGREN, K. E., WENNER, L. A. & PALMGREEN, P. (eds) (1985) *Media Gratifications: Current Perspectives* Beverley Hills, California, Sage.
ROWLAND, W. D. (1983) *The Politics of TV Violence: Policy uses of communications Research* Beverley Hill, California, Sage.
RUSHTON, J. (1979) 'Effects of prosocial television and film material on the behavior of viewers' in: L. Berkowitz (ed) *Advances in Experimental Social Psychology* Vol 12, pp 322-351 New York, Academic Press.
SCHRAMM, W., LYLE, L. & PARKER, E. B (1961) *Television in the Lives of Our Children* Stanford University Press.
SCHUCK, J & PISO, K (1974) 'Evaluating an aggression experiment by the use of similating subjects' *Journal of Personality and Social Psychology* 29(2), pp.181-188.
SHUTTLEWORTH, F. & MAY, M. (1933) *The Social Conduct and Attitudes of Movie Fans* New York, Macmillan.
SINGER, D. G., ZUCKERMAN, D. M. & SINGER, J. L. (1980) 'Helping elementary school children learn about TV' *Journal of Communication* 30, pp.84-93.
SINGER, J. L. & SINGER, D. G. (1981) *Television, Imagination and Aggression : a Study of Pre-schoolers* Hillsdale, New Jersey, Lawrence Erlbaum and Associates.
 - (1986) 'Family experience and television viewing as predictors of children's imagination, restlessness and aggression' *Journal of Social Issues* 42, (3), pp.107-124.
SMITH, M. L. (1980) 'Publication bias and meta-analysis' *Evaluation in Education* 4, pp.22-24.
SMITH, P. K. (1974) 'Ethological methods' in: B Foss (ed) *New Perspectives in Child Development* Harmondsworth, Penguin. pp.85-137.
SPIVACK, G., MARCUS, J. & SWIFT, M. (1986) 'Early classroom behaviors and later misconduct' *Developmental Psychology* 22(1), pp.124-131.
SPRAFKIN, J., GADOW, K. D. & KANT, G. (1988) 'Teaching emotionally disturbed children to discriminate reality from fantasy on television' *Journal of Special Education* 21(4), pp.99-107.
SPRAFKIN, J., SWIFT, C. & HESS, R. (1983) *Television: Enhancing the Preventative Impact of TV* New York, Haworth Press.
STEIN, A. H. & FREIDRICH, L. K. (1975a) 'The effects of television content on young children' in: A. D. Pick (ed) *Minnesota Symposium on Child Psychology* Vol 9. Minneapolis, University of Minnesota Press.
 - (1975b) Personal correspondence.
STROMAN, C. A. & SETTGER, R. (1985) 'Media use and perceptions of crime' *Journalism Quarterly* 62(2), pp.340-345.
TAMBORINI, R., ZILLMAN, D. & BRYANT, J. (1984) 'Fear and victimization' in: R. H. Bostrum (ed) *Communication Yearbook No 8* Beverly Hills, Sage. pp.492-513.
TANNENBAUM, P. (1971) 'Studies of Film- and Television- Mediated Arousal and Aggression: A progress report' in: G. A. Comstock, E. A.Rubenstein and J. P. Murray (eds). *Television and Social Behavior, Vol 5, Television Effects* Washington DC, US Government Printing Office.
TRACEY, M. (1984) 'Pouring cold water on the ketchup' *The Times* 25 February 1984.
TURNER, C. W., HESSE, B. W. & PETERSON-LEWIS, S. (1986) 'Naturalistic studies of the long-term effects of television violence' *Journal of Social Issues* 42(3), pp.51-73.
TURNER, C. W. & SIMONS, L. S. (1974) 'Effects of subject sophistication and evaluation apprehension on aggressive responses to weapons' *Journal of Personality and Social Psychology* 30, pp.341-348.
TYLER, T. M. & COOK, F. L. (1984) 'The mass media and judgement of risk' *Journal of Personality and Social psychology* 47, pp.693-709.
WALMSLEY, R. (1986) 'Personal violence' *Home Office Research Studies* No 89. London, HMSO.
WARTELLA, E. & REEVES, B. (1985) 'Historical trends in research on children and the media' *Journal of Communication* 35, pp.118-133.
WATKINS, L. & WORCESTER, R. M. (1986) *Private Opinions Public Polls* London, Thames & Hudson.
WELLS, W D. (1973) *Television and Aggression: a Replication of an Experimental Field Study* Unpublished manuscript. Graduate School of Business, University of Chicago.
WESTLAND, G.(1978) *Current Crises of Psychology* London, Heinemann.
WILLIAMS, T. M. (ed) (1986) *The Impact of Television: A National Experiment Involving Three Towns* New York, Academic Press.
WILLIAMS, T. M., ZABRACK, M. L. & JOY, L. A. (1982) 'The portrayal of aggression on North American Television' *Journal of Applied Social Psychology* 12, pp.360-380.
WINN, M. (1977) *The Plug-in Drug* New York, Bantam Books

WOBER, M. & GUNTER, B. (1982) 'Television and personal threat: fact or artifact? A British survey' *British Journal of Social Psychology* 21, pp.239-247.

- (1988) *Television and Social Control* Aldershot, Gower.

ZILLMAN, D. (1978) 'Attribution and mis-attribution of excitatory reactions' in: J. H. Harvey, W. J. Ickes and R. F. Kidd (eds) *New Directions in Attribution Research* Vol 2. Hillsdale, New Jersey, Erlbaum.

- (1979) *Hostility and Aggression* Hillsdale, New Jersey, Erlbaum.

- (1982) 'Television viewing and arousal' in: D. Pearl, L. Bouthilet and J. Lazar (eds) *Television and Behavior, Ten years of scientific progress and implications for the eighties* Washington DC, US Government Printing Office.

ZILLMAN, D. & BRYANT, J. (1986) 'Exploring the entertainment experience' in: J. Bryant and D. Zillman (eds) *Perspectives on Media Effects* Hillsdale, New Jersey, Lawrence Erlbaum. pp.303-324.

ZILLMAN, D. & JOHNSON, R. (1973) 'Motivated aggressiveness perpetrated by exposure to aggressive films and reduced by non-aggressive films' *Journal of Research in Personality* 7, pp.261-276.

III: PORNOGRAPHY: The Recent Debate

Dr Dennis Howitt

Introduction

The social effects of obscenity and pornography have been a relatively low-key issue in the United Kingdom in the years since the Williams Committee (Williams, 1979). However, in the USA researchers have been much more active and government has paid for a rather limited commission into the effects of pornography (U.S. Attorney General's Commission on Pornography, 1986). Unlike the American initiative of the late 1960's (U.S. Commission on Obscenity and Pornography, 1970), this new commission included no major funding for new research. Consequently it considered only the available social scientific research. The 1960's commission had failed to provide either a definitive answer on pornography's effects or the expected conclusions antagonistic to pornography. Richard Nixon, the president receiving the 1970's report, rejected it in apparent disbelief of its 'liberal' recommendations, asking how pornography could have no effect if great literature elevates mankind (Howitt, 1982)? The politics of the Commission, as well as its findings, have been the focus of various critiques (e.g. Cline, 1974; Eysenck and Nias, 1978).

The recent American Commission, however, was not feint hearted in its approach. For example, its request that 26 companies, including CBS and RCA, should disavow the commission's accusation of being involved in the sale or distribution of pornography in order to avoid being described as such in the commission's final report is indicative of this 'robustness' of style. Some organizations responded by suing the commission (Paletz, 1988). Considerable controversy was generated in the social scientific community and a somewhat muted, but clearly outraged response, was included in the *American Psychologist* (Wilcox, 1987). There is no intention to review this debate here - it adds little to clarifying the issues to describe the machinations of the commission (Einsiedel, 1988; Koop, 1987), the considerable internecine conflict among the social scientific community over data and their meaning (Brannigan, 1987; Christensen, 1986, 1987; Zillmann and Bryant, 1986, 1987a,b), and other apparent over-interpretations of psychological data by the commission. Vital when taking a 'cooler' look at the debate are the assumptions of the psychologists 'outraged' at the abuse 'scientific data'. Wilcox (1987) entitled his paper "Pornography, social science, and politics", perfectly reasonably, but curiously subtitled it "When research and ideology collide"!

Of course, the fundamental assumption, not unfamiliar amongst psychologists, is that what their profession promulgates is a 'value-free' account of human experience and action which contrasts markedly with the ideological content of non-psychologists accounts. This is not only arrogant beyond measure but also fundamentally misleading. Accounts based on Foucault's (1979) view of the 'professionalization' or 'disciplinization' of 'social problems' quite clearly demonstrate that put into the hands of professionals with a peculiar ethic common to that profession, does not necessarily lead to a neutral understanding of that 'social problem', but one which brings its own assumptions and ways of understanding which are value-ridden like other forms of human understanding. Howitt (in press) and others (Berridge 1984, Smart 1984) have described how the involvement of the medical profession in the development of British legislation on 'drug abuse' led to the treatment of drug users which we basically accept as 'right' today, but seems to clash fundamentally with the value framework of drug use in nineteen century Britain. These changes are both subtle in the sense that they are largely unnoticed by society but major in that they create radical shifts in societal understanding of matters.

Psychologists are familiar with the epithet 'medical model' being applied to the understanding and treatment of so-called 'mental illness' (eg. Szasz 1974)). They are also fully aware of the value implications of the 'medical model' with the 'distortions' that this brings to theory and treatment. However, they very rarely articulate the ideological position which underlies their own psychological research and theory. Certainly at times they will conceive of the debates of other researchers as ideologically motivated (e.g. the debates on racial differences in intelligence - Kamin, 1974) but usually not their own 'humble' day-to-day science. Zillmann and Bryant (1986) in the recent American controversy between pornography researchers and their critics incorporate accusations of the ideological basis underlying the critiques of their 'accusers' (Zillmann and Bryant use this term unflinchingly). Ideological problems in research are represented as if they are errors on the part of the researcher and that the 'true' science has no such worries. The failure to find the ideology in the science itself is revealed in Wilcox's (1987) contrast between research and ideology. It is almost as if psychology is the theology - ideology is for other professions.

Recent literature on the effects of pornography, it will be seen, can only be fully appreciated if the ideological assumptions of the discipline of psychology are understood clearly. Research, in itself, is only part of the story. The ideological context in which it is conceived and interpreted is also vital. It should be stressed that the point is not that psychologists as people have value positions and may be fascist, communist, liberal, humanitarian, and so forth. This is mundane. The point being made is that psychologists as psychologists operate within a discipline which has its own ideological characteristics. Like any other ideology, the effect is to routinely leave actions unquestioned which fit into the ideology. The ideological basis of psychology need not be unravelled in full here, but it includes the following components:

1. The training of psychologists leaves them 'objective' and minimally subject to value or ideological intrusions in their professional work.
2. There are ethics of research which are a distinct from the extra-professional 'social ethic'.
3. Psychologists along with other social scientists are the best able and the best trained to deal with 'objective' facts of social behaviour and experience.
4. The measures which psychologists use have an absolute reality and are not social in nature.
5. People are vulnerable to 'variables' and these 'variables' make them 'do' things.

Most of the above have been regular criticisms of psychology by psychologists and others (Reason and Rowan 1981). They have, however, been seen as largely relating to methodological issues rather than a professional ideology. Treating them as ideology encourages the view that they can be seen as the framework within which social issues are approached at every level by psychologists and not mere nuisances of method. The tone of moral outrage in psychology's response to the recent American commission seems to reflect the ideological core of the debate. Psychologists were not merely expressing the sort of annoyance which would have been appropriate, say, had a newspaper misreported a piece of their research, they were climbing onto the high moral ground of fairness, justice, rightness, honesty, and conscience. When Eysenck and Nias (1978) wrote:

> ... pornography and violence in the media are only symptoms of a much more widespread disease, namely a general loss of values, Christian, moral, or social. Being born of this general loss of values, it in turn feeds into it in a kind of positive feedback cycle. No great changes in social well-being should be expected even if the proposals here reviewed should be carried into effect, and no great disaster should be expected should nothing in fact be done. (p273)

they were probably misleading no-one about the value position they had adopted throughout their discussion of pornography and obscenity. It is clearly a personal view which cannot fully be supported by any social research. There is an element of take-it-or-leave-it which is not clouded by pretensions of professional objectivity which flaws much of the recent debate.

Background to the review

There has been a radical shift in the research on pornography in the last few years. The early research (circa 1970) had provided a pool of research findings on pornography and its effects which had scarcely existed prior to that date. However, it did have an air of desperation in that many different types of research method were brought to bear on the question. This is not surprising since the research of that time was commissioned in a hurry and the findings needed within months (U.S. Commission on Obscenity and Pornography, 1970). Inevitably the research paradigms used creaked somewhat under the strain, particularly as researchers, perhaps naively, fought for the ethical good standing of their research. As a result, none of the research looked directly at the effects of pornography on children though fewer qualms were expressed a matter of months later by a similar coterie of psychologists researching into media violence (Surgeon General's Scientific Advisory Committee on Television and Social Behaviour, 1972). One consequence was that the major focus of concern at the time, the effects of media on children, was left to the moral conscience and lay-psychological fears of media effects. Thus, the following assessment of the first-round of pornography research, only applies to adults.

While there is no doubt that sexual depictions are sexually arousing to many (Davis and Braucht, 1971; Mosher, 1971) this is in itself not at all surprising and would not be seen as reprehensible by the vast majority of people. There is sufficient evidence to warrant such effects of pornography and erotic materials proven. But this is not at all the same thing as saying that pornography and other erotic material causes sexual crimes or encourages 'perverted' sexual activity ... there has been little in our review to suggest such a link is proven. It is a little simplistic to assume that sexual deviance and sexual crimes are caused by a high degree of sexual arousal whether caused by pornography or not. (Howitt, 1982, p.120)

In the years since the first-round of pornography research there has been a shift in the ideological basis of the research. This is not the professional ideology but the significant ideological arguments about pornography underlying the social debate. During the first-round of pornography research the main ideological issues were those of maintaining conventional sexual morality which contrasted markedly with liberal notions of adults being free to choose for themselves. More universally accepted was the idea of protecting children which seems to have been subscribed to by all shades of opinion from the liberal to the most reactionary conservative. Remember that this latter ideological component also found no opponents among social scientists and psychologists - they simply did no research to challenge the notion either because they accepted the notion or had ethical reasons for avoiding such research.

During the early 1970s a further set of ideological concerns became more dominant.

Major steps in the women's movement's visibility and acceptance had been made. While many of these were to do with work and education issues, male aggression, including male sexual aggression, was represented as a major weapon in maintaining male social power. This ideological stance has elements which provide a common-purpose with the most reactionary conservative anti-pornographers, since pornography is seen by many feminists as a key cultural mechanism for encouraging sexual-aggression against women (e.g. Faust, 1980). Furthermore, the liberal conscience has to be troubled by the notion that male power has pornography at its roots, so that the freedom of women is partly limited because of the freedom to produce and distribute pornography. Several value systems thereby share a common objective - the attack on pornography. This lead to an ill-assorted moral army against pornography which includes in its ranks otherwise bitterly-opposed forces.

The second-round of pornography research seems to be substantially addressed to this question. Much of the research is couched in terms of male violence towards women and, in particular, male sexual violence. This has some fairly obvious advantages and some equally obvious drawbacks. The advantage is that it moves the ideological battle away from the difficult area of individual morality into the less problematic area of sexual violence which is more consensually unacceptable. In this sense there was the possibility that researchers would key their research into social policy much better than the first-round researchers had managed. Further advantages include the focus of concern being not children per se, but male psychosexuality. Adult females, thereby, become a legitimate, and relatively unproblematic focus for the researchers' attention. The research is protected from charges of being reactionary because it no longer is an issue of individual freedom since there is no moral freedom to harm others. Finally, the types of effects of pornography which need to be investigated are clarified considerably by the unifying ideology of the women's movement in comparison to what for the first-round researchers had been an unenviable range of complex choices from a range of conflicting ideological stances.

The disadvantages of this new research focus relate just as much to ideology. To study violence from a psychological point of view in order to assess the causal influence of pornography requires that measures of sexual violence are developed which are differentially affected by exposure to pornographic as opposed to non-pornographic material. The researcher is thereby left with a stark choice between confining measures to verbal ones of attitudes, intentions, judgements, and other evaluations, or encouraging men to demonstrate sexual aggression against women. The former immediately suggests the difficulty of whether verbal statements can be generalized to other forms of action, the latter raises the professional ethical difficulty of 'colluding' to encourage sexual aggression. It is impossible to imagine any experimental procedures which allowed the opportunity to aggress sexually against a female and which would not produce a considerable and embarrassing public debate. Probably for reasons which are closely related to this, researchers who have measured actual behaviour rather than responses to a questionnaire, have elected to study the effects of pornography on willingness to aggress against another person by using electric shocks made famous by Milgram (1974). This consists of instructing the individual to press switches which ostensibly result in a noxious electric shock being delivered to another person. No shock is actually delivered. While this technique has been criticised from an ethical viewpoint (Milgram 1974), it is so familiar in the psychological literature now that it attracts little comment. So sexual violence is equated, rightly or wrongly, with aggression as measured in this way. In this method, aggression is not discouraged - it is usually positively encouraged by the researcher. Whether or not this is analogous to male sexual aggression is clearly problematic since some have even questioned its relevance to social violence (Howitt, 1982). Being ideologically committed to this type of research, psychologists are more intent on keeping somewhat creaky research paradigms than exploring alternative ways of informing the debate.

The danger with any discussion of male sexual violence is that it is rather easy to drift into a manner of thinking which 'normalizes' or 'sanitizes' those acts. The psychological literature on pornography, by opting for approaches which concentrate on that aggression which seems acceptable for psychologists to measure in their experiments, implies that male sexual violence is similarly a relatively 'safe' affair. Reading the psychological literature on the effects of pornography encourages one to forget that male sexual violence includes elements of debasement, torture, and mutilation. Old ladies are murdered and raped after their deaths, women have their genitals burnt with cigarettes. Male sexual violence is not merely 'bottom pinching' and giving argumentative partners a spanking. It is all of these things and more. The following quotation from a rape victim in Burgess and Holmstrom's (1979) study reveals a lot:

> He had given me a good talk; he was a good con man and I was looking forward to having sex with him. I was horny and was feeling neglected, and I love my sex. He took me outside and down an alley and threw me on the ground. I asked him what he was doing - told him he didn't have to do it there if all he wanted was a screw ... I told him I wasn't a slut or whore that did it in an alley. It didn't matter... First he tried natural sex; then he insisted on oral sex. I didn't want to but he forced me - it was choke or take it. He wanted to [put it] in my mouth. I said no. He started getting real mad. The he said he was going to urinate on me.... He rammed his fist up me twice and he bit my breasts. Then he stood up and piddled all over me and said, "I feel better." ... He told me not to leave - he hit me and said, "You will do what I say." Then he left.

I didn't think he would come back. I started to get dressed and then he was back. He had another guy with him. The guy who raped me asked the other guy if he wanted me and the guy said, 'I want no part of it.' They both walked away. (Burgess and Holmstrom, 1979, p.15)

Male sexual violence as described by this woman seems light years away from the things psychologists have used as analogues of it in their research, often apparently without the slightest hint of equivocation about their choice. But the woman's experience was nothing unusual. (Hopkins, 1984)

Built into the 'theory' of pornography, not only the lay theory but also that of the psychological researchers, is a view of sexual violence which assumes that sexual arousal is the root cause of rape, along with myths about female sexuality. It is not at all clear that the rape requires the heightening of the sex drive to motivate it (Howitt, 1982):

> ... in working with identified rapists, both convicted and unconvicted, it becomes apparent that sexual desire is not the dominant motive in rape; nor is sexual frustration, for a variation on the myth that the victim has sexually enticed the offender is the view that the offender is a sex-starved male who must rape to relieve his sexual tensions and frustrations. The majority of rapists we worked with were married and engaged in regular sexual relationships within, and often outside of their marriages. Nor did many complain that their wives were inattentive or unresponsive to their sexual needs and interests...." Sometimes right after I had sex with my wife I would go out and rape someone. (Burgess and Holmstrom, 1979, p.23)

It inevitably becomes a serious criticism of much pornography research that it promulgates the very rape-myths that it assumes that pornography perpetuates. The image that the research presents of rape trivializes the degradation of women through rape by presenting it as lust.

Research on pornography and aggression

1 Interpersonal Aggression

With the problem of pornography research having been redefined as one of showing whether or not exposure to pornography increases the likelihood of aggression, the following are the major issues which one would expect researchers to address:
a) Do groups of people shown pornography compared to those shown non-pornographic material differ in their levels of aggression afterwards?

b) Is there evidence that this is an actual increase in aggression compare to levels prior to exposure to pornography?

c) As male sexual aggression against females is the focus of the ideological concern and the research issue, is there any evidence that the males are more influenced by pornography than females in this respect and that aggression is greatest for males against females than any other pattern?

d) What is it in pornography which produces these effects? Is it the violent content of the pornography or the sexual explicitness?

There are others, of course, but the above is intended not as an exhaustive list but merely a list which keeps an eye on the sorts of research which are typical of the rubric psychological. It hardly begins to ask questions about what sorts of themes, styles and contexts are the most 'dangerous'; or even how the messages of pornography manage to compete communicatively with contradictory messages from the women's movement, increased societal discussion of the nature of rape and the problems of the victim, the increased awareness of sexual abuse in the family which has tended to have a high media profile in recent years, the public outrage at lenient sentences to rapists and other counter-male sexual aggression cultural expressions. These are not trivial matters, merely matters made trivial by psychology's reluctance to approach them.

Theory in this area tends to yield to empirical work but one approach has an influence on conceptualizations of the pornography effects debate. This is Zillmann's excitation transfer model of communicative effects (Zillmann and Johnson, 1973). Stripped of its detail, the idea is very simple. It is merely that communicative stimuli, irrespective of their thematic content, vary in their ability to arouse people physiologically. The more physiologically aroused the individual, the more likely it is that the person will engage in actions which are determined by the social context, personality, and any other disposing factors. While this physiological 'high' can readily be appreciated as likely to encourage action, the model is problematic in this context for various extra-psychological reasons. The first and most important is that it matters not what causes the physiological arousal - a violent film, a sexy film, an exciting sporting programme, or even a quiz game - it is arousal which is crucial. The consequence of this arousal, however caused, will not be determined by the cause of the arousal but other factors which are not predictable from the original cause of the arousal. So a horror film would have the same ability as a pornographic film to result in the heightened likelihood of sexual behaviour should the conditions for sexual activity be present.

Such a theory makes issues like the moral or ideological content of the arousing material irrelevant. If thematic material is dismissed, then it becomes meaningless to even consider censoring or otherwise restricting material because of its specific content. What it implies is that media to be safe have to be 'boring' since anything else would risk the arousal which is seen as dangerous! (Howitt, 1982) Implications for policy stemming from research based on this model seem to melt away with careful examination. The model also can readily be seen as fitting in with the ideological commitment of psychology to a 'value-free' view of the world which requires the decontextualization of human action to keep the ideology from crumbling under siege from extra-professional moral and ideological forces.

The status of the excitatory transfer theory in the pornography research literature is largely as a means of ad hoc explanation of 'unexpected' research findings. Curiously it does not serve as a sign that researchers should equate their filmed materials in terms of arousal effects irrespective of content. The impression is created from reading the second-round pornography research that so long as the material meets with extra-psychological and ideologically based expectations, psychological theory can take a back seat.

Several studies have explored the influence of non-violent sexually explicit material on aggression. Typically erotic material caused heightened aggression in both male and female viewers (to the extent that the latter have been studied) if that erotica was arousing, whereas unarousing erotica calmed the angered brow and reduced aggression in the typical laboratory experiment (see, for example, Donnerstein et al, 1975). Zillmann and Bryant (1984), while following this standard pattern of research, 'massively' exposed their research subjects to pornography (Donnerstein, 1987) - meaning nearly five hours of sexual films over a six week period which is indeed several fold the usual dosage of a short snippet typical of these studies. Compared to control subjects who had seen 'neutral' films, the 'massively' exposed male and females actually showed lower levels when 'encouraged' to aggress against a person of the same sex. Donnerstein and Barrett (1978) examined male aggression against women following exposure to non-violent sexually explicit material. Not only did this produce no differences due to the type of material shown (a stag film or a wildlife documentary – no confusion intended), but even the men who had the most traditional attitudes towards women who might be expected to be imbued with a male-violence-dominance ethos were unaffected (Donnerstein and Hallam, 1978). Malamuth and Ceniti's (1986) study with more extensive exposure to sexually explicit material produced much the same outcome. Exceptions to this pattern are few, according to Donnerstein et al (1987). Leonard and Taylor (1983) studied the effects of 'permissive cues' or what might be better described as 'anything goes' comments apparently made by a woman to sexual or neutral slides. Perhaps not surprisingly, this woman when she gave high shocks to the males subjects and had made claims like she'd like to try the things in the sexual slides, received higher shock levels from the male subjects. The higher shock levels seem closer to moral condemnation than an effect of sexual images. Donnerstein and Hallam's (1978) finding that, given a second opportunity to aggress against a woman, subjects exposed to pornography had increased levels of aggression is perhaps an exception. However, its impact is reduced by the fact that the basic theoretical idea that repeated opportunities to aggress should disinhibit aggression did not emerge in a control and violent film condition.

At this point a feeling of cautious but rising disbelief might grow at the kinds of things psychologists 'do in the name of science'. One very important question has to be whether it is possible to carry out such studies as if they take place in a time-warped, amoral, culture-free test-tube. Quite what is the experience of taking part in this sort of research? Is there nothing strange about being shown sexually explicit films? Missing from the reports of this type of research is any discussion of this. After all, to be invited to visit the research laboratories of a University psychology department and then shown a snippet from a sexually explicit film is no everyday experience. Had this been a party at a stranger's home where these films were shown, we would be likely to have some moral stance and question the motives of the host – was this to be a partner swapping party? If then the host asked us to slap a perfectly willing young women who had made rude comments about our appearance, the moral crisis would probably reach a peak. Why then does this not happen in the psychologist's laboratory when people are asked to deliver painful electric shocks? Why are the researchers themselves apparently oblivious to the issue? The moral response of participants has been well-documented in similar research procedures (Milgram, 1974). However, the use of electric shock in communications effects research is a long tradition, not far short of its thirtieth anniversary. Considerable doubt has been cast on its ability to reveal substantial findings since it seems unduly responsive to minor variations in the expectations and prior experience of the participants (Howitt, 1982; Page and Scheidt, 1971). Exactly opposite findings emerge in virtually identical experiments although the participants seem loathe to hint that they were aware of the researcher's expectations (Page and Scheidt, 1971).

Researchers have not confined themselves to this style of research with sexually explicit material: they have extended the procedures to violent pornography. Curiously, the tone of the research seems markedly at odds with the social fact of sexual violence which it seeks to cast light on. For example, Donnerstein et al (1987) describe the features of violent pornography as follows:

> .... (1) A women (sic) is the victim of sexual coercion in a sexually explicit context. A man uses force against the women to obtain sexual gratification. (2) The depiction portrays a positive victim outcome. Rape is depicted as pleasurable, sexually arousing and beneficial to the female victim. (It) is this unique feature of violent pornography - the presentation of the idea that women find sexual violence arousing -that plays an important role in producing violent pornography's harmful effects. (Donnerstein et al, 1987, p.88)

While this seems very much to reflect social myths about sexual violence (c.f. London Rape Crisis Centre, 1984), it does not seem to meld together with the experiences of rape researchers. Not only does Donnerstein et al's pronouncement promote a rape-myth, it also does injustice to the rape research literature that could have helped conceptualization of the pornography research. For example:

> Rape is motivated more by retaliatory and compensatory motives than sexual ones; it is a pseudosexual act, complex and multidetermined, but addressing issues of hostility (anger) and control (power) more than desire (sexuality). (Burgess and Holmstrom, 1979, p.23)

There is nothing in this to suggest that rape is encouraged by the view that women, subject to a little force, will really enjoy what it is that they secretly crave in any case. The harsher reality clashes markedly with this. Killing one's victim before raping her is not doing the victim any sexual 'favours'. Forcing a beaten and raped victim to jab the penis of a drunk with the prongs of a fork does not fit this rape 'myth' particularly well. The pornography researchers seem to have in mind a 'tidied-up' view of rape which is closer to the 'stag' movies' view of rape than it is the "ignoring 'no' when it really signals 'yes' myth". Pornography researchers seem to have entered the pornographers ideological framework rather than one derived from concerned knowledge of rape. While if effects can be shown at the 'normal' edge of male sexual aggression, this is in some ways more important than demonstrating effects at the extreme limits of sexual violence and mutilation, that is not the only consideration. At its most basic, the question at issue is how does pornography research and rape research overlap? The pornography researchers seem to have their own concerns which are not particularly well-informed by knowledge of the social problem to which they ostensibly refer.

Donnerstein and Berkowitz (1981) differed little from the experimental research described above. The main difference was in terms of the films shown since these included not just a sexually explicit one but another showing a violent rape (sometimes at gunpoint, sometimes involving the victim being slapped). Male aggression on the shock-machine against and angering male was increased in both the sex and the violent sex conditions. Aggression against an angering female in these circumstances was enhanced only by the violent rape film. On theoretical grounds, they explored the effects of showing the victim of rape enjoying the act and eventually becoming a willing partner compared with an alternative version in which the female appeared to suffer and experience humiliation and disgust. An angering female was given greater shock levels after both of these versions than after the neutral and non-violent sex films. A study by Malamuth and Ceniti (1986) which features a longer term exposure to pornography found no similar effects due to long term exposure to pornography of a violent type. The conclusions one could draw from such studies should not be overstated, perhaps. The worrying aspect of it all is that the thematic content which contrasts 'rape myths of female pleasure' with a view more closely representative of the 'distress and humiliation reality' both produced heighted shock levels in angered subjects. This may imply the need for research into the decoding of themes in the viewing of pornographic materials if we are to take it seriously. Otherwise, as it stands, the implication is that no sort of coverage of sexually violent themes, irrespective of ideological and value concerns, can be made without risk of increasing the sexual violence which thematically that material opposes.

Of course, the above follows only if we take the research seriously. It has to be understood that there is not one jot of evidence which links this type of research finding with real-life sexual violence. Conjecture and surmise form the basis of any bridges. No one seriously believes, it would appear, that any of the men in the studies who aggressed against the female would leave the laboratory and commit some sexual assault. Such worries would, presumably, have led them to abandon the research as unethical at the slightest possibility of this. Indeed the researchers seem almost relieved when the more intensive studies involving 'massive' doses of pornography reveal no differences between the experimental and control subjects. While concern to express the effectiveness of 'debriefing' (explaining afterwards to the subjects what the research was about) would reflect a professional ethical stance (Donnerstein et al, 1987), it also reveals that the researchers believe that the subjects have their sexual and aggressive behaviour firmly under cognitive control - otherwise the debriefing would not work. If this is the case, any discursive elaboration about the undesirability of rape should effectively prevent it. Unfortunately, despite the generally prevailing media and otherwise culturally transmitted condemnations, this sort of violence is common enough.

In themselves, the studies either provide no evidence that sexual and sexually violent material increases aggression (rather than sexual aggression) or some evidence that aggression increases in the rather limited circumstances of immediately being able to aggress against a woman who has usually annoyed one considerably. It becomes a big conceptual jump from this to the many types of sexual violence which are perpetrated by men on women (and, let it be said, by males on males). This conceptual problem is made worse by the observation that women subjects of the experiments, where the research has been carried out, show virtually the same trends in the experiments (Baron, 1979; Cantor et al, 1978; Jaffe et al, 1974). Why are the women not the violent rapists? - they could humiliate men in much the same way. The answer is, of course, not to be found in the psychological laboratory but elsewhere.

One matter of particular curiosity value is the electric shock. It is equated as being a measure of aggression but seems not particularly responsive to the arousal of anger. So what is the relationship between the level of shock given and aggression? What determines the amount of shock given? Researchers using this sort of measure have shown that it is subject to evaluative overtones or evaluation (Milgram, 1974). That is, people tend to make judgements about what it is right or wrong to give by way of shock - in other words, they deliver shock by reference to a morality. It could be argued that in the context of pornography research participants have to make moral decisions about the amount of shock to give. However, the participant in the research has no properly socially grounded concept of what are appropriate levels of electric shock to administer to the other person. What the experimenter does is to shift the appropriacy of electric shock by changing the moral environment. Thus a researcher who shows violent pornographic films establishes a value framework for the research which is hardly gentle and kindly. Additionally, the participants in the research receive a fairly hostile treatment from another person (one of the experimenters). Finally, the subject is encouraged to aggress against the person who has treated him or her in a hostile fashion. Is it surprising that in these circumstances sometimes subjects choose to deliver high levels of shock? One might be more convinced of the research had they concentrated on a measure which is closer to the sexual violence for which the electric shock is taken to substitute. Perhaps the researchers should have measured the number of times the angering researcher spontaneously had his or her bottom pinched - but perhaps they didn't believe these things would happen in these circumstances.

2 Judgemental Decisions

Apart from the electric shock measures described above, recent research into the effects of pornography has involved what might be described as judgemental cum evaluative decisions. Superficially these complement the electric shock research since they are apparently far closer to the ideological issues than the electric current could ever be. Attitudes towards women, judgements as to the leniency of rape sentences, 'butch' male sexual viewpoints, and attitudes towards the women's movement can all be incorporated into research if a questionnaire can be put together to measure any of those things. If pornography is the theory or theology of rape, as is sometimes claimed, what better way of understanding the impact of pornography on ideology than to ask questions which deal with facets of this? Not only has one got closer to the social problem, one has got further from the ethical problem of encouraging male sexual violence against women. Notice, though, that the implication of this is that for psychologists ideology does not move the individual to action. While this is debatable, it is symptomatic of the generally low importance given to value positions by psychologists trying to understand human action.

Typical of this sort of research is the study by Zillmann and Bryant (1988). Some people taking part in this study were exposed to one hour of pornography per week for six weeks. At the end of this period they answered questions which dealt with various matters including those of a sexual nature. There was also a comparison group who had not seen the pornographic films. Those exposed to the pornography were significantly less satisfied with their sexual partner, the partner's appeal, the partner's sexuality, and the partner's sexual curiosity. Also, they saw family relations, faithfulness and sex with attachment as less important. Non-sexually related matters did not produce differences between the groups.

The big question to ask is what these differences mean. Zillmann and Bryant (1988) are rather matter-of-fact about this and do not make any grandiose claims. However, even granted this rare reticence on the part of American pornography researchers, what is the process underlying these differences? For one thing, the differences applied equally to male and females in various age groups. There was no sign that the pornography had a special appeal to the beliefs of the machismo male. Equally, it has to be pointed out, it is not really tenable to suppose that judgements of the sort made by Zillmann and Bryant's subjects are made in some absolute terms by accurate assessors. Completing any questionnaire involves considerable judgemental leeway since it raises questions of what to communicate to the researcher and what the researcher is getting at by the questions. In reaching these judgements the subject may take into account any factors which help anchor the judgement more solidly. In this respect, it is possible that by creating a climate which accepts the showing of pornography as part of research, the subjects are encouraged to be sexually honest. At the same time what the researchers have in mind as a upper peg for judgements about what constitutes a good and vigorous sexual relationship as well as an attractive partner are presented as clearly as they ever are. It is difficult to see, without these considerations, how pornography brings about an increase in dissatisfaction with the partner's affection! Zillmann and Bryant (1988) are apparently well aware of these anchoring processes when they point to other research of a non-pornographic nature which shows similar effects.

Other research by Zillmann and Bryant (1982), while having similar implications, has been, understandably, subject to considerable scrutiny given its subject matter. Essentially they showed some research participants relatively large amounts of stag film type pornography, others were control subjects. Subjects' estimates of frequencies of certain activities were compared with rates found in a sex survey. Brannigan (1987) summarizes the outcomes of the research and some implications as follows:

> ... consistency between the survey and the experimental estimates leads Zillmann and Bryant to suggest that "massive exposure to pornography thus could be said to correct distorted views of sexuality" by implicitly educating subjects to the extensiveness of oral sex in the population. However, estimates

by the massively treated subjects for such things as group sex, anal sex, sadomasochism and bestiality were higher than those in the survey data, which led the authors to suggest that posture appeared to "distort the perception" of sexuality. The logic of the argument is that different exposure levels create not just different attitudes but bad, i.e. distorted, attitudes. In other words, the ecological validity of the estimates made within the experiment is interpreted according to an external standard, and the massively exposed subjects are consequently shown to have acquired distorted views of reality. (Brannigan, 1987, p.185)

This strikes a familiar chord and warning signals. It has consistently been found (for a discussion see Howitt, 1982; Howitt and Cumberbatch, 1975) that human beings are very bad at making actuarial estimates of frequencies of 'deviant' activities. It is a rather meaningless question to ask what percentage of people do certain things. Indeed, it might be asked whether or not the researchers themselves would like to answer questions of a similar actuarial sort such as what proportion of couples make love in the bath? Not only have such estimates proved to be poor ones of social reality in other types of research, people are even very bad at judging the frequencies of activities reported in the media. That those shown pornography differed from those not exposed to it perhaps shows the desperation of the judgements rather than the conviction of the participants. It is far from clear that such judgements have any consequences for behaviour or any origins in personal experience (Cumberbatch and Beardsworth, 1977).

Even more alarm has been created by research which suggests that 'sexual callousness' results from exposure to pornography (Christensen, 1986; Zillmann and Bryant, 1982). Arising from Bryant and Zillmann's research programme already outlined, the major findings of this stage are that lower jail sentences for a rapist, lower support for the Women's Liberation Movement and greater sexual callousness towards women were found in the pornography compared with the control group. While the researchers tend to interpret these findings in terms boiling down to pornography making male sexual aggressiveness further acceptable, the findings may equally and less dramatically be merely artefacts of the difficulties of making judgements on questionnaires and the moral climate of the research for which these judgements are made. Having seen the pornography, the details of the rape described in the questionnaires might seem not as bad as otherwise but five years in prison is not a token sentence. Lower support for the women's movement might merely reflect that the films were not as extreme as the anti-pornography campaign might suggest. The moral climate of the pornography condition of the research might encourage honesty about sexual attitudes which appears, relatively speaking, as being increased callousness. Or, of course, participants may merely be playing a variation of the same research game as the researchers.

Certainly there seems more variability in the results of similar experiments than seems easily interpreted as causal influences of pornography - Check (1985) being in support but Malamuth and Ceniti (1986), Linz (1985), and Krafka (1985) producing no supporting evidence.

Here again the whole theoretical basis of this 'ideology of rape' research seems out of touch with the rape research literature. Clark and Lewis (1977) describe a rather different ideological basis in the psyche of the rapist radically unlike that which the sexual callousness idea would have predicted. The ideology is closer to that of romantic love!

> More commonly... the offender tries to see the situation in more generally acceptable terms.... Protestations of love are quite common. In one case, a woman of forty-four was asleep in her bedroom when attacked by a stranger fifteen years her junior. "During the struggle the assailant stated that he loved her.....All the time that he was trying this he kept saying that he loved her very much.

Another rapist, who attacked his victim in a heavily wooded area: "....fondled the victim's breasts and tried to kiss her, asking her if she loved him... This man shouted "goodbye" as he ran off when he was finished." (Clark and Lewis, 1977, p.102) The point is not that ideology is nothing to do with action, but that we cannot assume the nature of the ideology which leads to sexual violence as being as unproblematic as might appear from the psychological literature on pornography.

3 Other Effects of Pornography

Space does not allow a review of all the research, let alone the hints and suggestions which appear in the psychological literature alone. To some extent anyone familiar with the media violence literature can anticipate much of the 'theory'. Emotional desensitization to sexual violence shown in pornography echoes a similar theme in the media violence debate. That emotional reaction to violent pornography declines with repeated exposure to that material (Donnerstein et al, 1987) though is not easy to interpret (Howitt and Cumberbatch, 1975). However, desensitization of this sort is familiar to those in caring professions having to cope with stressful duties and sights. A nurse who cannot cope with the sight of blood is of little use. The nurse who emotionally adjusts is not thought of as in some way uncaring or unsympathetic, she is seen as coping and professional. There is no conceptual link between emotional adjustment (desensitization) and morality. Likewise, we do not for one minute assume that the rape victim who comes to terms with her emotional crisis brought on by the attack has in some way become 'immoral' because of this adjustment.

76

Conclusions

This review of the pornography literature has tried to set it within a judgemental and ideological framework. There seems little doubt that ideologies of different sorts both combine and clash to produce the issues and means of study adopted by psychologists researching pornography. It is impossible to see the activities of psychologists as simply those of technicians who answer important questions concerning social issues. Not only do they personally inevitably have value positions and ideological allegiances, so does their profession. At times they appear naive when faced with the reality they are trying to explain because of these ideological constraints.

There does not seem to be compelling unequivocal evidence that allows any strong conclusions about pornography based on research. Ideological factors and the sheer complexity of the problem do not encourage any faith that further research will answer the questions posed by the available literature. The desire for proof in a causal sense seems to conflict with a properly socially-contextualized interpretation of the problem.

But this is not to say that certain research could not prove useful. However, new research should be wary of falling into any of the ideological traps. The idea that pornography reduces moral standards has been displaced by the concern about male sexual aggression in the more recent literature. But both are alike in that they assume pornography is an issue because it makes people do things. Are the effects of pornography on actions the basis for serious concern about pornography? If pornography does not have the claimed effects, would there be a case for freely broadcasting it? Possible future areas of research might include:

1. What sorts of material consensually should not be broadcast and what are the time and other parameters which might constrain this?
2. What sorts of depictions are justified by what sorts of thematic contexts for broadcasting?
3. What is the influence of broadcasting authorities on judgements of acceptable materials for broadcasting? That is, are the public influenced by the moral and ideological ethos of the broadcasting organizations in their views of the material?
4. What are the means by which families deal with issues arising from sexually related material being viewed in the family context?
5. What is the public's confidence in and expectations of media organizations in relation to sexual material?
6. What can be done to enhance the mutual understanding of the public and broadcasters in respect of sexual material?
7. How do broadcasters and regulatory bodies actually construe and deal with the issue?

8. Can over-control of sexual material be counterproductive and undermine the broader objectives in the public's view?

9. How can the media promote an effective understanding of the problem of sexual violence?

None of these questions, and many others which could be raised, require the traditional concerns of researchers and critics of broadcasters about the media making people do bad things. They are more to do with the way in which morality and ideology are constructed, the role of social institutions in this process and providing the broadcasting authorities with an understanding which is more responsive to society than merely stamping the seal of appointed authority on the issue.

KEY REFERENCES

BARON, R.A. (1979) 'Heightened sexual arousal and physical aggression: an extension to females' *Journal of Research Personality* 13, pp.91-102.

BERRIDGE, V. (1984) 'Drugs and social policy: the establishment of drug control in Britain 1900-30' *British Journal of Addiction* 79, pp.17-29.

BRANNIGAN, A. (1987) 'Pornography and behaviour: alternative explanations' *Journal of Communication* 37 (3), pp.185-9.

BURGESS, A.W., & HOLMSTROM, L.L. (1979) *Rape: Crisis and recovery* Bowie, Maryland: Robert J. Brady Co..

BUSS, A. (1961) *The Psychology of Aggression* New York, Wiley.

CANTOR, J., ZILLMANN, S., & EINSIDEL, E.F. (1978) 'Female responses to provocation after exposure to aggressive and erotic films' *Communication Research* 5, pp.395-413.

CHECK, J.V.P. (1985) 'Hostility towards women: some theoretical considerations' In G.W. Russell (ed.) *Violence in intimate relationships* New York, Spectrum.

CHRISTENSEN, F. (1986) 'Sexual callousness revisited' *Journal of Communication* 36 (1)., pp.174-184.

- (1987) 'Effects of pornography: the debate continues' *Journal of Communication* 37 (1), pp.186-8.

CLARK, L.M.G., & LEWIS, D.J. (1977) *Rape: the Price of Coercive Sexuality* Toronto: The Women's Press.

CLINE, V.B. (ed.) (1974) *Where Do You Draw the Line? an Exploration into Media Violence, Pornography, and Censorship* Provo, Utah: Brigham Young University Press.

COMMISSION ON OBSCENITY AND PORNOGRAPHY (1970) *The Report of the Commission on Obscenity and Pornography* New York: Bantam.

COMMITTEE ON OBSCENITY AND FILM CENSORSHIP. (1979) *Report* Cmnd 7772. London: H.M.S.O.

CUMBERBATCH, G., & BEARDSWORTH, A. (1977) 'Criminals, victims & mass communications' in E. Viano (ed.) *Victims and society* Washington: Visage Press.

DAVIS, K.E., & BRAUCHT, G.N. (1971) 'Reactions to viewing films of erotically realistic heterosexual behaviour' in *Technical Reports of the Commission on Obscenity and Pornography* Vol. 8. Washington D.C: U.S. Government Printing Office.

DONNERSTEIN, E., & BARRETT, G. (1978) 'The effects of erotic stimuli on male aggression toward females' *Journal of Personality and Social Psychology* 36, pp.180-8.

DONNERSTEIN, E., & BERKOWITZ, L. (1981) 'Victim reactions in aggressive erotic films as a factor in violence against women' *Journal of Personality and Social Psychology* 41, pp.710-24.

DONNERSTEIN, E., DONNERSTEIN, M., & EVANS, R. (1975) 'Erotic stimuli and aggression: facilitation or inhibition' *Journal of Personality and Social Psychology* 32, pp.237-44.

DONNERSTEIN, D., & HALLAM, J. (1978) 'Facilitating effects of erotica on aggression against women' *Journal of Personality and Social Psychology* 36, pp.1270-7.

DONNERSTEIN, E., LINZ, D., & PENROD, S. (1987) *The Question of Pornography: Research Findings and Policy Implications* New York: The Free Press.

EINSIEDEL, E.F. (1988) 'The British, Canadian, and U.S. pornography commissions and their use of social science research' *Journal of Communication* 38 (2), PP.108-121.

EYSENCK, H.J., & NIAS, D.K. (1978) *Sex, Violence, and the Media* London: Maurice Temple Smith.

FAUST, B. (1980) *Women, Sex and Pornography* Harmondsworth: Penguin.

FOUCAULT, M. (1979) *Discipline and Punish* Harmondsworth: Penguin.

HOPKINS, J. (ed) (1984) *Perspectives on Rape and Sexual Assault* London: Harper and Row.

HOWITT, D. (1982) *Mass Media and Social Problems* Oxford: Pergamon.

- (in press) *Britain's 'substance abuse policy': realities and regulation in the United Kingdom.*

JAFFE, Y., MALAMUTH, N., FEINGOLD, J., & FESHBACH, S. (1974) 'Sexual arousal and behavioural aggression' *Journal of Personality and Social Psychology* 30, PP.759-64.

KAMIN, L.J. (1974) *The Science and Politics of IQ* Potomac, Md: Lawrence Erlbaum.

KOOP, C.E. (1987) 'Report of the surgeon general's workshop on pornography and public health' *American Psychologist* 42 (10), pp.944-5.

LEONARD, K.E., & TAYLOR, S.P. (1983) 'Exposure to pornography, permissive and non-permissive cues, and male aggression toward females' *Motivation and Emotion* 7, pp291-9.

LONDON RAPE CRISIS CENTRE (1984) *Sexual Violence: the Reality for Women* London: The Women's Press.

MALMUTH, N., & CENITI, J. (1986) 'Repeated exposure to violent and non-violent pornography: likelihood of raping ratings and laboratory aggression against women' *Aggressive Behaviour* 12, pp.129-37.

MILGRAM, S. (1974) *Obedience to Authority* New York: Harper and Row.

MOSHER, D.L. (1971) 'Psychological reactions to pornographic films' in *Technical Reports of the Commission on Obscenity and Pornography* Vol. 8. Washington, D.C: U.S. Government Printing Office.

PAGE, M. & SCHEIDT, R. (1971) 'The elusive weapons effect: demand awareness, evaluation apprehension, and slightly sophisticated subjects' *Journal of Personality and Social Psychology* 20, pp.304-18.

PALETZ, D.L. (1988) 'Pornography, politics, and the press: the U.S. Attorney General's Commission on Pornography' *Journal of Communication* 38 (2), pp.122-136.

REASON, P. & ROWAN, J. (1981) *Human Enquiry: A Sourcebook of New Paradigm Research* London: John Wiley.

SMART, C. (1984) 'Social policy and drug addiction: a critical study of policy development' *British Journal of Addiction* 79, pp.31-9.

SURGEON GENERAL'S SCIENTIFIC ADVISORY ON TELEVISION AND SOCIAL BEHAVIOR. (1972) *Television and growing up: the impact of televised violence* Washington, D.C: U.S. Government Printing Office.

SZASZ, T.S. (1961) *The Myth of Mental Illness* New York: Harper and Row.

U.S. ATTORNEY GENERAL'S COMMISSION ON PORNOGRAPHY. (1986) *Final Report* Washington, D.C: U.S. Department of Justice.

WILCOX, B.L. (1987) 'Pornography, social science, and politics: when research and ideology collide' *American Psychologist* 42 (10), pp.941-943.

ZILLMANN, D., & BRYANT, J. (1982) 'Pornography, Sexual Callousness and the Trivialisation of Rape' *Journal of Communications* 32 (4), Autumn pp.10-21.

- (1984) 'Effects of massive exposure to pornography' in N. Malamuth, & E. Donnerstein (eds.) *Pornography and Sexual Aggression* New York: Academic Press.

- (1986) 'A response' *Journal of Communication* 36 (1), pp.184-8.

- (1987a) 'A reply' *Journal of Communication* 37 (3), pp.189-92.

- (1987b) 'A response' *Journal of Communication* 37 (3), pp.187-8.

- (1988a) 'A response' *Journal of Communication* 38 (2), pp.185-192.

- (1988b) 'Pornography's impact on sexual satisfaction' *Journal of Applied Psychology* 18 (5), pp.438-53.

ZILLMANN, D., & JOHNSON, R. (1973) 'Motivated aggressiveness perpetuated by exposure to aggressive films and reduced by non-aggressive films' *Journal of Research in Personality* 7, pp.261-76.

SUBJECT INDEX

NAME INDEX

Poindexter, 18, 28
Postman, 10, 28
Poulos, 22
Pratt, 35
Price, 48, 79

Ramsdell, 18
Rawlings, 34, 53
Reason, 10, 18, 50, 63, 80
Redfern, 51, 57
Reed, 31, 56
Reeves, 5, 29, 33, 58
Reinhardt, 48, 56
Reiss, 35, 53
Rogers, 4, 14, 23, 24, 28
Rokeach, 3, 4, 17, 27
Rosengren, 4, 28, 49, 58
Ross, 33, 53
Rowan, 63, 80
Rowland, 28, 50, 58
Rubens, 45, 57
Rubin, 49
Rubinstein, 7
Rushton, 22, 28, 48, 58

Sanchiro, 31, 56
Scheidt, 37, 57, 70, 80
Schramm, 5, 8, 9, 28, 42, 58
Schuck, 58
Scott, 14, 28
Sears, 34, 54
Sebastian, 41, 57
Seggar, 16
Selnow, 23
Settger, 32, 58
Shaffer, 35
Shang, 17, 27
Shatter, 55
Shotland, 35, 40, 57
Shuck, 37
Shulman, 9, 28
Shuttleworth, 33, 58
Signorielli, 2, 12, 13, 14, 16, 18, 28, 31, 55
Silverstone, 11, 29
Singer, 8, 23, 24, 28, 39, 40, 48, 50, 52, 54, 58
Smart, 62, 80
Smith, 36, 48, 54, 58, 79
Solomon, 8, 29
Solzhenitsyn, 11
Spivack, 46, 58
Sprafkin, 17, 24, 25, 27, 28, 32, 33, 47, 48, 50, 52, 55, 56, 58
Stein, 38, 40, 41, 56, 58
Stephenson, 35, 56
Sterling, 10
Stipp, 35, 45, 56, 57
Stovard, 14
Stroman, 18, 28, 32, 58

Surgeon General's Scientific Advisory on Television and Social Behavior, **80**
Svennevig, 9, 27, 29
Swift, 10, 46, 48, 58
Szasz, 62, 80

Tamborini, 32, 58
Tankard, 3, 29
Tannenbaum, 38, 58
Taylor, 11, 29, 49, 69, 80
Teevan, 43, 57
Thangavelu, 28
Thomas, 40
Thrasher, 33, 54
Tracey, 10, 11, 27, 46, 58
Truman, 26
Turner, 47, 58
Tyler, 32, 58

U.S. Attorney General's Commission on Pornography, 61, 80

Van der voort, 10, 27
Vidmar, 17
Vince, 5, 28, 42, 55

Walder, **54**
Wallack, 20
Walmsley, 31, 58
Walter, 46
Wartella, 5, 29, 33, 58
Warzak, 19, 29
Watkins, 28, 31, 56, 58
Watson, 27
Wells, 40, 58
Wenner, 49, 58
Werner, 3, 4, 28, 29
West, 41, 57
Westland, 37, 48, 58
Wharton, 44, 55
Whitaker, 56
Wilcox, 61, 62, 80
Willhoit, 18
Williams, 15, 32, 44, 56, 58, 61
Winn, 10, 29, 44, 58
Winnick, 11, 29
Witherspoon, 28
Wober, 13, 14, 15, 19, 21, 29, 32, 50, 55, 57, 59
Woon, 27
Worcester, 31, 58
Wynberg, 9, 29

Yuker, 19

Zabrack, 32, 44, 56, 58
Zielman, 13
Zillman, 27, 38, 49, 58, 59
Zuckerman, 48, 58

THE BROADCASTING STANDARDS COUNCIL

In May 1988, the Home Secretary announced the establishment of The Broadcasting Standards Council (BSC) to consider the portrayal of violence, of sex, and matters of taste and decency in broadcast and video works. Lord Rees-Mogg was appointed Chairman at the same time.

The Role of the BSC

The BSC has been established initially on a non-statutory basis, pending legislation during 1989/90. During this pre-statutory phase the Council's role is to:

i)   draw up, in consultation with the broadcasting authorities and the other responsible bodies in the broadcasting, cable and video fields, a code on the portrayal of violence and of sex and standards of taste and decency;

ii)   monitor and report on the portrayal of violence and of sex, and standards of taste and decency, in television and radio programmes received in the UK and in video works;

iii)   receive, consider and make findings on complaints and comments from individuals and organisations on matters within its competence and ensure that such findings are effectively publicised;

iv)   undertake research on matters such as the nature and effects on attitudes and behaviour of the portrayal of sex and of violence in television and radio programmes and in video works;

v)   prepare an annual report, which the Home Secretary will lay before Parliament and publish.

In addition, the Council is consulted by the Government on developments in Europe on the future regulation of transfrontier broadcasting.

Members of the BSC

There are eight Members of the Council:

Lord Rees-Mogg, Chairman. Former Editor and Director of The Times, Vice-Chairman of the BBC Board of Governors and Chairman of the Arts Council of Great Britain. He is Chairman and proprietor of Pickering and Chatto Limited and a Director of GEC.

Miss Jocelyn Barrow, OBE, Deputy Chairman. A former BBC Governor, Senior Lecturer in Education, Vice Chairman of the Campaign Against Racial Discrimination and Member of the Community Relations Commission.

87

Mr Richard Baker, OBE. He began broadcasting for the BBC in 1950 and continues regularly to present programmes on BBC television and radio.

Dr Jean Curtis-Raleigh is Consultant in Adult Psychiatry at Queen Mary's University Hospital, Roehampton.

Mr Alf Dubs, former Labour MP for Battersea South and for Battersea. He is currently Director of the British Refugee Council.

Dr R. Brinsley Jones, was a University Lecturer and Warden of Llandovery College. He is a member of the Board of the British Council, a University of Wales Examiner and Governor.

Rev Charles Robertson is Parish Minister, Canongate (The Kirk of Holyroodhouse).

The Rt Rev William J. Westwood, The Bishop of Peterborough. A former member of the Press Council, IBA Panel of Religious Advisers and the BBFC Video Consultative Council.

Lord Rees-Mogg was appointed for a five year period, the other Members for three years.

Senior Staff of the BSC

The Council is served by a staff complement of thirteen.

Senior members of staff include:

Colin Shaw, Director. Former Chief Secretary to the BBC Board of Governors, Director of Television at the IBA and Director, Programme Planning Secretariat at the Independent Television Companies Association. He was appointed as the Director of the BSC in November 1988.

David Houghton, Deputy Director. Served in the Research, Police, Prison, Fire, and Broadcasting Departments of the Home Office before assisting Lord Rees-Mogg in establishing the BSC. He was subsequently appointed Deputy Director.

Dr David Docherty, Research Director. Former research fellow at the Broadcasting Research Unit.

Katherine Lannon, Press and Programmes Officer

Clare Reynolds, Assistant Press and Programmes Officer.

The Broadcasting Standards Council
5-8 The Sanctuary
LONDON SW1P 3JS
Telephone: 01-233 0544
Fax: 01-233 0297

ABS 3191